Memoirs of Fatemeh Pakravan

Harvard Iranian Oral History Series
VI

Memoirs of Fatemeh Pakravan

Wife of General Hassan Pakravan: Army Officer, Chief of the State Intelligence and Security Organization, Cabinet Minister, and Diplomat

Editor

Habib Ladjevardi

Iranian Oral History Project
Center for Middle Eastern Studies
Harvard University
1998

Copyright 1998 by the President and Fellows of Harvard College

ISBN 09-32885-19-5

Library of Congress Catalog Card Number 98-072971

Printed in the United States of America

PUBLISHED BY THE
CENTER FOR MIDDLE EASTERN STUDIES
OF HARVARD UNIVERSITY
AND DISTRIBUTED BY
IBEX (IRANBOOKS, INC.)
8014 OLD GEORGETOWN ROAD
BETHESDA, MD 20814 USA
TELEPHONE: 301-718-8188
FAX: 301-907-8707

Contents

Preface	1
Background of Fatemeh Pakravan	3
Brief Biography of General Pakravan	4
Mrs. Pakravan's Memoirs	5
Note on the Interview	10
About the Project	11
Spelling of Proper Names	12
Memoirs of Fatemeh Pakravan	13
First Session: 3 March 1983 (12 Esfand 1361)	13
General Pakravan's Early Education	17
Coup of 19 August 1953 (28 Mordad 1332)	18
Formation of the State Security Organization	19
General Teymour Bakhtiar	21
Pakravan as Chief of Security Organization	23
Uprising of 5 June 1963 (15 Khordad 1342)	29
Ayatollah Khomeini Under Detention	36
Saving the Life of Ayatollah Khomeini	38
Assassination of Prime Minister Hassan-Ali Mansour	44
Pakravan Becomes Minister of Information	45
Shah's Reaction to Pakravan's Execution	47

Second Session: 7 March 1983 (16 Esfand 1361)	50
Her Own Background	50
Working at the Najmiyeh Hospital	52
Fathollah Pakravan	55
Years at Iranian Airways	57
Doing Social Work	58
National Tourist Organization	63
Ambassador to Pakistan (1966–68/1345–47)	68
Second Term at the Najmiyeh Hospital	69
Ghavam al-Saltaneh	79
General Haj-Ali Razmara	80
Former Queen Soraya	81
Atmosphere at the Court	86
Queen Farah, the Early Years	87
Princess Ashraf	90
Queen Farah, the Later Years	93
Hossein Ala	98
Dr. Manouchehr Eghbal	101
Dispute over Doubling the Price of Fuel	103
Rise of the Technocrats	104
Doubling the Price of Domestic Oil Products	106
Assassinations of the 1970s (1350s)	106
General Nematollah Nassiri	110
Public Life of the Security Chief's Wife	112
The Charles Jourdan Incident	114
Appointment to the Ministry of Court	117

Pakravan's Audiences with the Shah	120
The Last Days of the Monarchy	122
Arrest of Amir-Abbas Hoveida	125
Arrest of General Pakravan	130

Appendixes

1: List of Narrators	135
2: Project Staff	142
3: Libraries Holding the Collection	143
Index	145

Preface

The Iranian Oral History Project was launched at the Harvard Center for Middle Eastern Studies in the autumn of 1981/1360.[1] The project provides scholars studying the contemporary political history of Iran with primary source material consisting of personal accounts of individuals who either played major roles in important political events and decisions from the 1920s to the 1970s (1299–1359) or witnessed these events from close range.[2]

To select the narrators, we prepared a list of major players in Iranian politics. This included the names of four former chiefs of the State Intelligence and Security Organization (SAVAK).[3] By the time we began our interviews, however, none of the former chiefs was alive. The organization's first head, General Teymour Bakhtiar (1957–61), had been assassinated by his own former agents in 1970. The second director, General Hassan Pakravan

---

[1] Throughout this work, the first date refers to the Gregorian calendar and the second to the Islamic solar calendar based on the migration of the Prophet Mohammad from Mecca to Madina on 16 July 622 A.D.

[2] See Habib Ladjevardi, *Reference Guide to the Iranian Oral History Collection* (Cambridge, Mass.: Harvard Center for Middle Eastern Studies, 1993).

[3] SAVAK is the acronym for *Sazman-e Ettelaat va Amniyat-e Keshvar* (State Intelligence and Security Organization).

1

(1961–65), was executed in 1979 by the revolutionary court. The third and fourth chiefs, Generals Nematollah Nassiri (1965–78) and Nasser Moghadam (1978–79), were also executed by the new regime.

We therefore turned to the second tier of SAVAK officials, and interviewed General Hassan Alavi-Kia[4] who had worked closely with the first two security chiefs. At the end of every interview we always asked the narrator for names of others in his or her field who could offer further insight into events we had discussed. When I put this question to General Alavi-Kia, he strongly recommended Mrs. Fatemeh Pakravan, the widow of his former chief. The general considered her to be extremely intelligent, perceptive, and knowledgeable woman who would be of great value to our endeavor.

When I met Mrs. Pakravan, I learned that she and her husband had developed a partnership unusual for Iranian couples of their generation. Even though he did not talk of state secrets with her, he nevertheless discussed his own concerns and solicited her advice. As a result, during their four decades of marriage, she was aware of many important events, decisions, and discussions. Moreover, her own career outside the home and her great interest in public affairs enabled her to remember details of these observations, which she candidly told us. We

---

[4] General Hassan Alavi-Kia, born in Hamadan on 12 January 1912, was deputy chief of SAVAK (1957–62/1336–41), and head of the European branch (1962–67/1341–46). See his memoirs in the Harvard Iranian Oral History Collection.

are grateful to her for giving us an intimate glimpse into the inner circle of Iran's political elite and providing us with the context in which events took place.

Background of Fatemeh Pakravan

Fatemeh Pakravan was the daughter of Javad Farifteh and Olya Brilevski, who was half Polish and half Russian. Her parents met in Tiflis, Georgia, in 1917, during the Russian revolution. After her parents married, they moved to Iran, where in Rasht, in 1918/1297, Fatemeh was born. Sometime later, the family moved to Tehran, enabling Fatemeh to attend Jeanne D'Arc, a French school.

When Fatemeh was only ten years old, her parents divorced and she and her sister, Narguesse, accompanied their father to France. Initially she was enrolled at Pension Saint Honoré d'Eylau, a Paris convent, and then at a public school. Upon completing high school, she pursued paramedical studies. On her return to Iran, she met Captain Hassan Pakravan in the summer of 1940, and married him the following February.

Mrs. Pakravan maintained a diverse career while raising four children. This practice was highly unusual for an Iranian woman in the 1940s. She was director of the Najmiyeh Hospital and head of maternity at the Bank Melli Hospital, teacher of French at the Institute for Foreign Languages of Tehran University, head of planning and development of the National Tourist Organization, and an active member of the Red Lion and Sun Association (Iran's Red Cross).

Brief Biography of General Pakravan

Hassan Pakravan, son of Fathollah and Emineh, was born in Tehran on 4 August 1911 (13 Mordad 1290). His father held many high government posts, including governor of Khorasan and ambassador to Italy.[5] His mother, partly of European descent, was a professor at the University of Tehran. She was awarded the prestigious French Prix Rivarol, which the French government gives to foreign authors who write directly in French.[6]

As a child, Pakravan accompanied his parents to Cairo, where his father was appointed diplomatic agent.[7] There, he received his primary education at the Lycée français. He was

[5] Fathollah Pakravan was appointed consul general in Constantinople in 1910/1289. From there he went to Egypt as diplomatic agent. He returned to Tehran in 1925/1304 and was appointed director of the Russian and Turkish section in the Ministry of Foreign Affairs. In July 1926/1305 Pakravan was made vice minister of foreign affairs, and promoted to acting minister in November 1928/1307. He was appointed minister in Rome in December 1928/1307 and ambassador to the Soviet Union in February 1931/1309, accredited to Finland and Estonia as minister in 1932/1311, recalled from Moscow in February 1934/1312, and appointed governor-general of Khorasan, a post he retained until 1942/1321. He was then sent to Italy as ambassador, staying in that post until his retirement.

[6] She was the daughter of Hassan Khan, an Iranian diplomat. Her mother was Alice von Herzfeld, daughter of Stephan von Herzfeld, an Austrian military officer and friend of Maximilian whom he joined in Mexico.

[7] Not yet independent, Egypt did not receive ambassadors [FP].

Preface

then sent to Liège, Belgium where he attended high school and university. Pakravan then studied at the artillery school in Poitiers, France, and the Ecole d'Application d'Artillerie in Fontainebleau.

Pakravan began his career at the Tehran Military Academy, where he taught artillery. He then served in a number of military, political, and diplomatic posts including adjutant in the Intelligence Department of the Second Division, military attaché in Pakistan (1949–50), chief of army intelligence (1951–53), military attaché in India (1954–57), deputy chief of the State Intelligence and Security Organization in charge of external affairs (1957–61), deputy prime minister and chief of the State Intelligence and Security Organization (1961–65), minister of information (1965–66), ambassador to Pakistan (1966–69), ambassador to France (1969–73), and senior counsellor to the Ministry of Court (1974–79).

Mrs. Pakravan's Memoirs

Mrs. Pakravan's informative and often fascinating memoirs describe many aspects of life in Iran. She gives first-hand accounts of important events and colorful descriptions of major personalities of the period 1940–79. In one section, she sketches the behavior of visitors to the Najmiyeh Hospital, Tehran's most prominent hospital in the 1940s, and describes her attempts at introducing modern modes of behavior similar to those practiced in Europe: "People used to come in the hospital with their carpets, their charcoal stove or kerosene stove—I mean the entire family: children and grandchildren. They would spread their carpets and really [have a] picnic there, smoke cigarettes, speak aloud, come and go any time of day or night."

Mohammad Mossadegh was the trustee of the Najmiyeh Hospital and thus her first employer. While she admired him as an individual, she disapproved of his statesmanship: "In his physical aspects, he reminded me of a French writer. He was really *grand seigneur*—very courteous, very, very nice, [and] spoke French beautifully." She asserts that during his term as prime minister (1951–53), "Dr. Mossadegh . . . governed practically all the time under martial law. This is something again that people have forgotten. Also it was actually Dr. Mossadegh who [planted] the seed of what came to be known as SAVAK."[8]

With regard to Queen Soraya, the shah's second wife, she says, "I didn't like Soraya, because I found her very, very cold, very distant." She confirms that the shah was very much in love with Soraya. She also reveals that Soraya did not like to live in Iran. "Several times she tried . . . to persuade the king to abdicate and go live abroad."

Princess Ashraf is someone of whom Mrs. Pakravan speaks with some sympathy. She recounts a story, told her by a friend,

---

[8] She is referring to the establishment of a committee composed of chiefs of police, gendarmerie, and army to coordinate security throughout the country.

Preface

which sheds some light on the princess's desire in later years to amass wealth. In 1953, when Prime Minister Mossadegh expelled Princess Ashraf from Iran, the princess lived in a small hotel in Paris. According to the friend, the princess had put a few pieces of very cheap jewelry on her bed and said, "You know, I was kicked [out] like a servant from [my] house. I wasn't even allowed to take any of my things. This is all I was able to bring with me. But, I swear in front of you that if ever the situation turns back, I shall become a very, very, very rich person."

One of the more fascinating segments of her memoirs is the description of her husband's weekly luncheons with Ayatollah Khomeini in 1963, when the ayatollah was under house arrest. According to the general, "The ayatollah used to say in this very flowery Eastern way, '*Timsar* [General], I count the days until we reach the day of our luncheon.'" He described the ayatollah as, "very handsome. He had extraordinary presence, a power of seduction. He had a great charisma." They talked about religion, philosophy, and history. The general found "his ignorance in history and philosophy [to be] unbelievable." He also found him to be very ambitious and secretive. So much so that "it made my hair stand on end. It was frightening," he told his wife.

She confirms the well-known story that her husband saved Ayatollah Khomeini's life in 1963. "He was condemned to death and my husband was very, very upset by that." Pakravan felt that his execution would anger the common people of Iran. "He knew that the population of the country is not its elite." He presented his argument to the shah. Once he had convinced the shah to allow him to find a way out, he called on Ayatollah Mohammad-Kazem Shariatmadari, one of the senior religious leaders of Iran, and asked for his help. Ayatollah Shariatmadari suggested that Khomeini be made an ayatollah. "So, they made a religious decree which . . . was taken by my husband and Seyyed Jalal Tehrani to the shah."

During the last year of the monarchy many events contributed to its eventual fall in February 1979. Mrs. Pakravan describes an incident in which the bodyguard of the wife of a SAVAK official killed a bystander at the Charles Jourdan shoe shop in Tehran. She calls the incident "one of the causes of the revolution."

During the autumn of 1978, a number of attempts were made to save the monarchy. These included changes of cabinet, the liberalization of the political atmosphere, and the arrest of former government officials. In this regard, Mrs. Pakravan relates how the shah and the queen decided to arrest Prime Minister Hoveida.

Mrs. Pakravan gives us a sense of the atmosphere at the court and around the shah during the last months of the monarchy. According to her, people would telephone her husband, or come to their house and say, "Please, you must go to the shah. You are the only person to whom he will listen."

Preface

And General Pakravan, somewhat dejected at not being engaged by the shah, would say, "No. No. No. No. The shah doesn't see me. He never receives me. I am quite put aside." As a result of his wife's insistence, however, General Pakravan requested an audience and was granted one immediately. There have been many reports regarding the psychological condition of the shah during his last days in Iran. Mrs. Pakravan's account confirms these reports. As she says, "After that [audience], the shah saw my husband very often. [My husband] said, 'Whenever, I see the shah, I have the impression that he is like a drowning man who sees me as some safety to which to cling.'"

In the final section of her memoirs, Mrs. Pakravan provides details of the arrest, imprisonment, and execution of her husband by the revolutionary court. General Pakravan was taken from his house to an unknown destination. When his son tried to contact him, he was told that the general was "not arrested at all. He is the guest of the ayatollah." But in fact he was imprisoned shortly after his arrest.

According to a fellow inmate, a few days before his execution, General Pakravan had smiled and said, "It's funny. I've never lived in such conditions even in the army—in such complete *dénuement* [destitution]. I know what's going to happen to me. It will be the machine gun, but I've never felt so [peaceful]."

Harvard Iranian Oral History Collection

Note on the Interview

I recorded the memoirs of Mrs. Pakravan in two sessions lasting a total of three and one-half hours on 3 and 7 March 1983 (12 and 16 Esfand 1361) at her apartment in Paris. I met Mrs. Pakravan for the first time on the day of the interview. General Alavi-Kia, whom I had recorded earlier, not only suggested that I interview her, but also made the introductions. The interviews took place in the living room of her tastefully decorated apartment in the Sixteenth. During our sessions no one else was present.

Since Mrs. Pakravan's memoirs are being published during her lifetime, we sent a copy of the transcript to her so that she could correct factual errors and provide missing data and add new information or comments, if she desired. Her additions are included in footnotes, marked with her initials.

When the final draft of the manuscript was ready, we sent her the first few pages including the title page in order to ensure that the facts were correct. On the title page below the text introducing her husband she wrote, "It is O.K. except that in a very rich life of service and devotion to duty, he is remembered only as head of security where he stayed less than four years—and where he applied his intelligence [and] human qualities to . . . this organization—which at the start in 1956 was never meant to become the criminal SAVAK. It should be remembered that the fathers of this organization, justly criticized in later years, were the United States of America with the help

Preface

of Israel."

About the Project

Since its inception, the project has recorded the memoirs of 133 individuals, comprising approximately 900 hours of tape and 18,000 pages of transcript, at a cost of over $800,000. The project was funded by a large number of supporters including the National Endowment for the Humanities ($300,000) and the Ford Foundation ($50,000). The collection embodies the most comprehensive chronicle of eye-witness reports of modern Iran by some of the key figures who defined her history. Microfiche of the collection has been purchased by libraries of major universities in Canada, England, Germany, France, and the United States. A more complete description of the project can be found in *The Reference Guide to the Iranian Oral History Collection*.[9]

In the autumn of 1995, the Steering Committee of the Harvard Center for Middle Eastern Studies approved a plan to publish a number of the memoirs in order to make them more readily available to the academic community and to publicize the existence of the collection among specialists. During the last three years, six volumes have been published including the *Memoirs of Fatemeh Pakravan*. They are listed inside the back cover. The published memoirs are identical to the original transcripts, except for minor editorial changes. Also footnotes

---

[9] See footnote 2, p 1.

have been added to introduce individuals and places and to explain events.

Spelling of Proper Names

The system of transliteration used in this book is a modified version of that introduced by Farideh Tehrani in *Negligence and Chaos: Bibliographical Access to Persian-Language Materials in the United States* (Metuchen, NJ: Scarecrow Press, 1991). In line with that system, we have followed the spelling adopted by Iranians for their own names. Consequently, because few Iranians use the letter *q* to denote ق, preferring instead the letters *gh*, we have spelled قاسم as *Ghassem* and not *Qasem*. We have followed the same approach in case of vowels. Thus, in the name محمود the letters *ou* have been used instead of *u*, resulting in *Mahmoud* and not *Mahmud*.

Geographical names have been spelled according to *Webster's New Geographical Dictionary*. Accordingly, the letter *q* has been used for the city of *Qom*. In case of compound names, we have used the hyphen, i.e. Mohammad-Reza and Ghavam-Shirazi.

Habib Ladjevardi
September 1998

Memoirs of Fatemeh Pakravan

First Session: 3 March 1983 (12 Esfand 1361)

HL: Mrs. Pakravan, please begin this session by giving a brief background of yourself and your late husband, General Hassan Pakravan.

FP: What kind of background do you want? Do you mean my studies and things like that?

HL: Whatever you think would be of interest to others.

FP: Well, it's not really interesting. I was educated in France from childhood and [subsequently] went back to Iran. I did what they call paramedical studies, and on my return to Iran I became the head of a hospital which belonged to the Mossadegh family.

HL: Najmiyeh Hospital?

FP: Najmiyeh Hospital. I met my husband and married him in 1941 [1320]. He was a captain at the time. We had four children. And what is important, I think, is that after a stay in Pakistan where my husband was the first military attaché of Iran, and following a long, very long, visit that the late

[Mohammad-Reza] Shah made to Pakistan, my husband started what I would call a political-military career. That means that he was appointed chief of G-2, General Staff[10] which at that time was different from what it became later on. Every service had separate and independent—more or less—headquarters.

He worked there, first as assistant and then as chief [even] though he was much too young. At the time—in 1950 [1329]—he must have been thirty-nine [years old]. He [had been] a full colonel for only one year. He accepted the job first because as an officer he thought that he must not [question] decisions, and also because he had a very idealistic view of intelligence work. For him intelligence work never, never, never was something consisting only of spying on people and trying to catch them [doing] something wrong. It was to know exactly who was trying to subvert different classes or even the country; and to somehow, whether by convincing, by talking to them, or by [fulfilling] human needs, try to change their opinion.

I remember when he was chief of G-2, it coincided with the period when Mr. Mossadegh was [both] prime minister and minister of defense.[11] That's something people keep on forgetting, that Dr. Mossadegh as minister of defense governed practically all the time under martial law. This is something again that people have forgotten. And also that actually it was

---

[10] G-2 was the intelligence arm of the military [FP].

[11] After his resignation over control of the Ministry of War and the 30 Tir 1331 (21 July 1952) uprising, Mossadegh took personal charge of the ministry, renaming it the Ministry of Defense.

Dr. Mossadegh who set the seed of what came to be known as SAVAK.

HL: Did he?

FP: Yes. You know at the time the Persian Communist Party, called the Tudeh, was extremely active, the Russians had hardly left Azerbaijan, and the so-called republics they had instituted in Kurdistan and Azerbaijan were extremely strong. Mossadegh was well aware of the danger of these people infiltrating every activity in the country. So, he established the National Council of Security, presided [over] by himself and [composed of] the heads of the three services (army, navy, and air force), the police department, the gendarmerie, and the chief of G-2—that was my husband. Of course, my husband was very junior and he never opened his mouth. Well, his impression of Dr. Mossadegh will be for another time.

But I remember asking Gholam-Hossein Mossadegh,[12] the son, "How come whenever something happens—there is trouble in town—your father immediately changes all the military chiefs, but he never touches my husband? Does he know that Colonel Pakravan is my husband? You'd better ask him." Then he told me the next day, "No. He [Dr. Mossadegh] didn't know he was your husband, but he said, 'I will never change him. I know him [to be] absolutely loyal to the shah. I know also that he has absolute respect for the laws of the country. And because

---

[12] See Dr. Gholam-Hossein Mossadegh's memoirs in the Harvard Iranian Oral History Collection.

of that, I know he'll never start something against me, the legal, legitimate prime minister of the country.'"

In 1952 [1331] there already must have been plans to [overthrow] Mossadegh. My husband was not in [on] these plans, but he was worried. In his job he naturally knew [of] rumors and things like that. The shah didn't confide in [my husband]. The shah was extremely enthusiastic about him, but after a while, it seemed [to the shah] that [my husband] was not—how shall I say—[in favor of] security for security's sake. [He was] for something more—bigger. I wouldn't say [he was a] liberal, because in America the word liberal has a very bad meaning, however, in French it has not. In French, it means a man who is a democrat.

Anyway, my husband was terribly worried and insisted that I and the children—at that time I had only three children—should go to France, where my father was established. I refused, but he insisted.

After a while, he came to Paris on the invitation of the French General Staff. [At about the same time], he received word that he was appointed assistant military attaché [in Paris]—until August or July. I don't remember [the exact month], you know, the 28th of Mordad,[13] when the Mossadegh government was overthrown. Very shortly after that, my husband was called back to Iran.

---

[13] 19 August 1953.

HL: When did he come to Paris as a military attaché?

FP: He came to Paris in May 1953 [1332]. There was a long-standing invitation from the French General Staff. Because my husband, [held a] high military rank and was entirely French-educated, he was very well known among the [French] army. (Actually, I have to complete that somehow.) But the [army] chief of staff, General Baharmast, refused to let him go—although he pretended to be like a father [to him].

Eventually I appealed to Gholam-Hossein Mossadegh, and I said, "Look here. Everybody goes to Europe at the expense of the government. Now my husband has been [serving] here for twenty years. He has a very, very difficult job. He's tired. He's demoralized. He's invited. It doesn't cost you anything." So [his father, Mohammad] Mossadegh, was very nice and let him go.

General Pakravan's Early Education

Now I shall tell you about my husband's education. He went to Cairo [where] his father was the ambassador in Egypt for ten years. [There] my husband received his education at the French school. Then he went to the Lycée français.

HL: In Cairo?

FP: In Alexandria and Cairo. [Then] he went to a high school in Liège, Belgium. After high school, he went to the university to train [as an] engineer. But his father was very close to Reza Shah and wanted him to go for military studies.

Reza Shah was trying to modernize the Persian army and wanted the sons of good families to be trained as officers for this army. So my husband went to an artillery school in Poitiers, [France] and from there to a higher artillery school in Fontainebleau (which doesn't exist anymore). It was called Ecole d'Application d'Artillerie. He graduated from there and went back to Iran to the Cadet Academy [دانشکده افسری], where he was commanding a—what you call—*ateshbar* [آتشبار], gun. He trained young officers, young cadets, for artillery. So, all the friends he had in these two schools, they were progressing in their careers and they had left the army. But still, my husband had many, many friends.

Coup of 19 August 1953 (28 Mordad 1332)

Anyway, he came to Paris in May 1953 [1332]. It was twenty years since his last trip. There he learned in August that there was this uprising, which I am still not absolutely convinced was only the work of the CIA. It's now the custom, and even the fashion, to say that in 1953 [1332] the shah was reestablished on his throne through the CIA. Probably [he] was, but there was also great popular feeling [in favor of the shah]. Of that I'm absolutely sure, although I wasn't there. I'm saying that from information I received.

Anyway, in September [1953/1332] my husband was recalled to his job [chief of G-2]. The conditions of his job had changed. Because already there were some convictions, some belief, that one has to be very, very, very strict about security and information. Not that my husband wasn't, you see. I don't want this to be misunderstood, but [there was a tendency to be more security conscious] in a more technical, less human way. I don't know, really, because my husband never said anything about his job except things that he could tell [every]one.

After a few months [as chief of military intelligence] he resigned in the spring of 1954 [1333]. He wanted even to resign from the army, but the shah, who liked him very much, said, "I know Pakravan likes to be abroad. I give him, I propose him, a job as military attaché in Switzerland, Pakistan, or India." My husband chose India because it was silly to return to Pakistan after a few years and Switzerland was much too expensive and the army officers were not paid that much. So we went to India and we liked it very much—both of us.

Formation of the State Security Organization

In October of 1956 [1335], he was called to Tehran where he stayed two weeks and came back very enthusiastic. My husband was a very, very enthusiastic man. It doesn't mean that he was stupid. He was certainly a most learned and good man and very intelligent. I will show you, for instance, what one of the great French journalists, André Fontaine,[14] has written about him in his book. Many people know that [my husband] was

---

[14] Editor of the French daily, *Le Monde* [FP].

someone very exceptional.

Anyway, he came back [to India]. He was very enthusiastic. He said, "We're returning to Iran." I said, "Oh, no. No. No. No, please. We still have two more years here." He said, "I'll tell you why. They have set up a new organization which is fantastic. And they're offering me the head of the foreign department of this organization."[15] I didn't know what it was. He said, "It's a [wide-ranging] organization that will look after security and information. Security and information go together. You cannot have security if you don't have information." He also said, "Besides, I am a little bit cut off from everything [here]. After all, I'm an officer, and it's so pleasant to work with brother officers." He still had some illusions at the time.

Anyway, we went back [to Tehran]. Alavi-Kia must have told you that the organization had two departments: the internal and the external. Hassan was [to be in charge of the] external. The [two departments] were completely separate from each other—that means there was a real wall. Many times when the question arose of this and that, my husband really didn't know. He did know in a general way, but he didn't know for sure, because [the two departments] did not exchange information—[unless it was] something that my husband knew was important for the internal situation or for the external

---

[15] On 3 October 1956 (11 Mehr 1335) *Ettelaat* reported that the cabinet approved a decree providing for the establishment of the State Intelligence and Security Organization (SAVAK).

Memoirs of Fatemeh Pakravan

situation.

General Teymour Bakhtiar

[This] was the time I met Teymour Bakhtiar.[16] I found him a very shy person.

HL: Really?

FP: Really! I remember we invited him, for he wanted to meet some people. I invited him to dinner at our house which was very modest, but not as modest as his. He was always like that, like a little boy. He gave you the impression of the wild tribal chieftain, although he was educated. But I don't think his education had changed him as a person. You know, sometimes education is very superficial. Sometimes it thoroughly changes a person, because it gives reflection and a philosophical point of view. Anyway, he was very shy with ladies. Although from what we hear, he wasn't.

I wouldn't know, really, how he came to resign. I can only tell you what my husband said to me. Bakhtiar and my husband had gone to London for a meeting. They had these meetings of branches of RCD[17] all the time—here, there, and everywhere.

---

[16] General Teymour Bakhtiar, military governor of Tehran (1953–57/1332–36), deputy prime minister and chief of SAVAK (1957–61/1336–39), was exiled to Europe (1962/1340), retired from the army (1962/1341), and charged with corruption (1967/1346). He was tried *in absentia*, his properties were confiscated, and he was condemned to death (1969/1348). He was attacked by agents of SAVAK in Iraq on 9 August 1970 (18 Mordad 1349). He died two days later.

[17] RCD is the acronym for Regional Cooperation for Development, an organization composed of Turkey, Iran, Pakistan, the United

While [in London], they went to a doctor, a heart specialist in Harley Street called Dr. Courtney Evans. It was [at] a time when the pressure of work led to heart attacks for many people everywhere. You always heard that so-and-so had a heart attack. So they went and had a check-up. Later [my husband] said, "You know, [a check-up] doesn't mean a thing, because you can have [one and be considered] perfectly all right and [then] go through the door and drop dead."

Anyway, from what my husband told me, and I don't have any reason to disbelieve him, at that time Bakhtiar started to worry about a possible heart attack. Now, I don't know, in view of what happened later, if it was just a smoke screen, or he really was [concerned]. Perhaps it was [a combination of] the two.[18]

HL: They both had this check-up or just Bakhtiar?

FP: Both of them. Yes. My husband was very amused. He said Dr. Evans examined him for a full hour. Then he came back to Iran and a heart specialist said in five minutes exactly the same thing as Evans had said: "You know, I cannot prevent you from having [a heart attack], but what you can have is certain regime in your life. You must stop smoking, you must not put on weight, and you must have exercise. If you do that, you'll lessen the risk [of a heart attack]." Anyway, it was my Kingdom, and the United States.

[18] After his resignation, he was exiled to Europe where he joined forces with the opponents of the shah. He then moved to Iraq, where he based his campaign against the monarchy.

husband who had the heart attack later.

So [my husband and General Bakhtiar] came back, and from that moment—it must have been in the early 1960s [1340s]—Bakhtiar started to say, "Oh well, I am fifty-nine." Or perhaps sixty. I don't remember. I have a very bad head for dates. Bakhtiar pretended to confide in my husband. He said he was very impressed by my husband. Many people were, you know. My husband was very easily approachable and a very courteous and charming person. His mother used to say, "In Iran, real virtue is admired although not practiced." And [my husband] was admired, because everybody said he was so wonderful, because it was easier to admire than to practice—honesty, all this and that. [These compliments] used to make him laugh, because he had a great sense of humor.

Eventually, Bakhtiar said, "You know, I am fed up with this job. What's the point? You work, you work, you work, and then suddenly you drop dead and all you have done is as nothing. I must resign." At one time even—I think, I'm not sure—he said, "I would like to be ambassador in some quiet place."

Pakravan as Chief of Security Organization

Anyway, my husband was away in Turkey for CENTO[19] or RCD—something like that—when suddenly he was recalled.

---

[19] CENTO is the acronym for the Central Treaty Organization, initially called the Baghdad Pact.

(Now, at the time the chief of G-2 was a certain General Kia,[20] who had a very, very bad reputation. And what I'm saying now to you, I think it was my husband who told me.) My husband was recalled. I remember that it was so complicated to come back from Turkey. He had to go to Europe to catch a plane to come [to Tehran]. [After he returned], he was kept waiting for forty-eight hours before the shah received him. And he said the shah told him, in a very business-like manner, "Bakhtiar is resigning.[21] I wanted to make changes in the upper level of the army. My intention was to make you chief of G-2 in place of Kia. But now that Bakhtiar has resigned, I want you to take his place." And my husband, I must say, was overcome because it was a terrible responsibility.

HL: Wasn't he eager to have this job?

FP: No. He wasn't. And so he asked for a short period of reflection. And the shah said, "All right. Take time and give me your answer, but don't be too long in deciding." So, my husband came home, and discussed it with me. He said, "You know, I have a conviction that I can do much good in this job. It all depends on my team, who is going to work with me, [and] whether I have a free hand." He was walking up and

---

[20] General Haj-Ali Kia. See his memoirs in the Harvard Iranian Oral History Collection.

[21] General Teymour Bakhtiar resigned his position as deputy prime minister and chief of the State Intelligence and Security Organization on 15 March 1961 (24 Esfand 1339) due to "ill health" and was replaced by General Hassan Pakravan.

down, up and down, all the time. And I said, "You know, the most important thing is [if] you can really be of use, then okay." Of course, in the last resort he took the decision himself.

He asked for an [audience] and told the shah, "Your Majesty. You should know me. You know my ideas. You know my education. You know my convictions. I don't have to define them to you, but one of my convictions is that you cannot ensure security in a country through fear. You can only ensure it by giving security to people—and to the poorest. Not to the upper class, because they [will] always manage to settle and to organize their life, but [to] people who have absolutely no recourse to anywhere."

And the shah said, "What do you mean?" He said, "Well, I think that [improved] economic welfare will [strengthen] this question of security. If people are happy, if people are satisfied—and they don't want much. They want the means to earn their living, the means to educate their children, the means to look after their well-being and health—that's all they want. People are very modest." The shah said, "All right. It's a point of view. I'll give you the means to apply your methods and we'll see."

So, first of all he reorganized the Security and Information Organization. He said there was no point in having an external and an internal department, because the two were so [intertwined]. "We have to have all the information [in] a pool." Then, of course, he established a fantastic library and insisted that all the officials from the [lowest rank] to the highest, [must] read. Also they [were given] training in history, in philosophy, in security—all the subjects that could be related to ensuring the security of the country.

Of course, later on he became a little bit bitter in his humor. One of the young men [Parviz Sabeti] he had educated—[who] was wonderful [and] admired [by everyone]—became a horrible fellow under Nassiri.[22] [He had become] so horrible that I refused to sit beside him at a dinner. I asked my husband, "But how come? He was one of your trainees. He was so wonderful. Everybody loved him." He said, "*moqtaziyat-e zaman*" [مقتضیات زمان], expediency of the time]. It can be translated in this way: that you act in a certain manner when its fashionable. When it's out of fashion, you go after the new fashion. So if under Pakravan it is democracy and humanity, and [under] another one it is oppression and torture, you go after [the new fashion].

One of the things my husband used to say to me after he left [the State Intelligence and Security Organization was], "In three thousand years—in all the history of Asia—I am practically the only fool that never practiced torture." He never boasted. I

---

[22] General Nematollah Nassiri, commander of the imperial guards (1950s/1330s), chief of national police (1960–65/1339–44), deputy to Prime Minister Hoveida and chief of SAVAK (1965–78/1344–57), ambassador to Pakistan (1978/1357), was recalled, arrested and imprisoned during the last months of the monarchy, and executed by the revolutionary court (1979/1357).

don't want to give you the impression that he was boasting. Everything I'll tell [you] from him are just facts that he recognized.

He used to laugh and say, "My prisons are like four-star hotels." And it was confirmed, because I remember Allahyar Saleh[23] was sick and he was taken from prison to the hospital. [Saleh] used to say, "I don't want to see anybody except my dear General Pakravan." You know, he was respected and all that.

Anyway [my husband] started, for instance, an economic [improvement initiative]. One was to establish the *ostandar-e banader* [استاندار بنادر]. That was the governorship of the Persian Gulf ports and harbors. You couldn't call them ports and harbors, because they were just small fishing [villages].

He said, "We cannot have [the Persian Gulf ports] dependent [upon] another governorship, because they're not interesting. They're poor. They produce nothing. They're very primitive

---

[23] Allahyar Saleh, son of Seyyed Hassan Khan Mozaffar al-Mamalek (civil servant). A graduate of the American College in Tehran; he was employed as a secretary in the American Legation in Tehran (1920s/1300s); judge and public prosecutor, Ministry of Justice; director of opium monopoly, the tobacco monopoly, and head of customs, Ministry of Finance; minister of finance (1943/1322), member of the Election Supervisory Board (1943/1321), head of trade mission to India (1943–44/1322–23), minister of justice (1944/1323 & 1945/1324)), minister of state (1945/1324), minister of the interior (1945–46/1324), minister of justice (1946/1325), Sixteenth Majles deputy from Kashan, minister of the interior (1952/1330), ambassador to the United States (1952–53/1331–32), leader of the National Front, and Twentieth Majles deputy from Kashan.

people. They have small tribal organizations which fight each other all the time."

He [established the new governorship] because, as a chief of G-2, he was at one time political officer and civil governor of Bushehr. At the time the British were in Bushehr. They had their political agent there. At the time it was Geoffrey Prior. My husband was horrified to see in what conditions the people lived. That was when he was very, very young. That was, let me see, I was expecting—in 1945 [1324]. So he had seen [the region] from close up. He saw the fighting and the killing between the tribes. I'm sorry to go back all the time.

HL: No. No. It's fine. It's not a problem.

FP: In the early 1960s [1340s] there was a terrible earthquake around Qazvin. And we had a friend [named] Mary Gharagozlou who was half-American. Her mother was American and her father Iranian. Mary had been one of the important landowners in Hamadan before the agrarian reform. She was married to a Bakhtiari chieftain. She knew practically all the languages of the tribes. She was an extraordinary woman and an agriculturalist. When this earthquake happened, she saved the day for many, many peasants. It being autumn, she knew that the most important thing was not to give them kettles, pots, and pans, but to plow the land and to sow [the seeds] to ensure the next harvest. Otherwise, they would die of hunger.

Because she did that in such an intelligent way, my husband said, "Mary, I'm going to entrust to you the well-being of all the tribes." But he didn't want her to be attached to his organization. So she was attached to the Ministry of Housing, the head of which was Dr. Nahavandi,[24] who liked and admired my husband very much. They started building very nice houses with bazaars and mosques in the south of Tehran which was horrible before. People were living in hovels. It was very bad.

Uprising of 5 June 1963 (15 Khordad 1342)

And so it went until the Khomeini business started. It started in a very insidious way—by preaching in the mosques. Photographs of this man—he was in Tehran—[were] everywhere. I remember asking a family who had—not exactly an antique shop—[but] a junk shop. People used to go there and find something. I said, "Why do you put up all these pictures?" He said, "He's someone to imitate"—*marja' taqlid* [مـرجع تقلیـد]. I'd never heard that before. I said, "You don't need to imitate someone. If you live in your religion, if you practice a good life, you don't need to imitate him." That was the feeling, you know.

[At the same time], women were [stared] at, because they

---

[24] Houshang Nahavandi, minister of development and housing (1964–68/1342–47), chancellor of Pahlavi University (1968–71/1347–50), chancellor of Tehran University (1971–76/1350–55), chief of Shahbanu Farah's Secretariat (1976–78/1355–57), minister of science and higher education (1978/1357), arrested by the Bakhtiar government, escaped from prison and fled to Paris (1979/1357). See his memoirs in the Harvard Iranian Oral History Collection.

were not wearing the veil. Unfortunately, what started also a little bit later was the mini-skirt for ladies. Iranian women [in some sense] were scattered-brained. [They adopted] any fashion that came. One day it was the skirt sweeping the floor. The next day [they] were practically naked.

Anyway, my husband saw these religious preachers, Falsafi,[25] Shariatmadari,[26] and whoever. I remember at one time they were to come every day. There was this enormous attendance in our house. My husband talked to them and he said, "Please, if you have anything, why don't you go to the proper authorities? Why madden people and try to subvert them and to prod and all that? What are you going to gain by that? I have the authority to stop you, but don't let me use the means that are at my disposal. Please remember. You are Iranians. This is your country. Please think about the results of your present action which is absolutely thoughtless. What do you think you will achieve? What do you think you will obtain?"

Of course starting with Khomeini and the rest, who thought they would gain something, the thing that made [them] mad was the agrarian reform. Here again I have to say something which is not directly related to [the preceding]. Arsanjani[27] did

---

[25] Mohammad-Taghi Falsafi, born 1910 (1289), preacher.

[26] Ayatollah Seyyed Mohammad-Kazem Shariatmadari, born in Tabriz in 1904/1283 was a leading source of imitation for Shiites since 1961/1340. He was formally stripped of his rank of ayatollah al-ozma, however, after the discovery in 1982/1361 of a plot against Ayatollah Khomeini which allegedly had his support.

[27] Hassan Arsanjani, son of Seyyed Mohammad-Hossein (cleric

a lot of wrong to the country, because he was the one—not much after Mossadegh—who really sowed the seed of class hatred in Iran when he said, "bloodthirsty landowner." [Once] that friend of mine, Mary Gharagozlou, rang me up and said, "This is *malek-e khunkhar* [مالك خونخوار] speaking." This is the blood-thirsty landowner speaking.

[The government was] not very clear about this agrarian reform. They started by saying it would only be the big landowners, the big absentee landowners. Then, after a few months, it was the [turn of the] middle ones. So it went step by step to the point [where] a man who had two acres of land was practically sure to be kicked off his land.

The mullahs and the religious people were afraid for what they called religious endowments, because most of the sanctuaries and shrines were extremely rich. For instance Imam Reza,[28] Shah Abdolazim,[29] Shah Cheragh[30]—all the shrines,

and born in Arsanjan, Fars) was born in Tehran in 1922/1301. Upon graduation from Tehran University, he began publication of *Darya* in 1944/1323. He was a founding member of Ghavam al-Saltaneh's Democrat Party of Iran (1946/1325), elected to the Fifteenth Majles (his credentials were rejected), deputy to Prime Minister Ghavam (1952/1331), secretary-general of the Freedom Association [جمعیت آزادی] (1957-58/1336-37), arrested for alleged plot against the government (1958/1337), minister of agriculture (1961-63/1340-41), ambassador to Italy (1963-67/1342-46). He died from a heart attack at the age of 47 on 31 May 1969 (10 Khordad 1348).

[28] Shrine of Imam Reza in Mashhad.

[29] Shrine of Shah Abdolazim in the city of Rey.

[30] Shrine of Shah Cheragh in Shiraz.

they were extremely rich, because people donated land, money, jewels, precious antiques, and rugs. They would donate anything. And actually the mullahs took advantage of all these donations. In some cases where it was too obvious, like Mashhad, they had hospitals, orphanages, and all kinds of charitable activities. Still the greatest part of all these benefits went to themselves. I think they didn't even spend for the upkeep of the shrines. I think it was the government—the endowment organization, *Oqaf* [اوقاف], who did that.

So, little by little we reached June 1963 [Khordad 1342] when it was the [month of] Moharram and they had the religious processions. This really invited people to rise. It was not the revolution, but the beginning of it. The army was alerted and put in the street. The [organizers of the processions] put small children in front so nobody could do anything. And, under the pretense of religious processions, they went and really broke everything in sight—even the telephone booths, the benches, the shops. Everything, anything, anything.

Naturally, the government had to react. And my husband did something which was certainly wrong from a Persian point of view. Sometimes he forgot that he had to deal with Orientals—Orientals not in the sense of Far [Eastern] Orientals, but people from the East whose minds do not evolve in the same way. I don't say it's wrong. I mean that you have to talk their own language. Why Khomeini succeeded this time [was] because he spoke the language of the people. And why the other gentlemen didn't succeed [was] because they spoke in a too complicated way, too literate way.

Now when I say [my husband] made a mistake, [it is] because even the intellectuals, even the educated people didn't understand what he [intended]. He spoke on the radio and what he said is written exactly on my mind. After the army took over, there were of course plenty of reprisals. Even though he had not ordered [the crack-down], he said, "Everything is my fault, because for months and months I spoke. Most of my activity consisted of speaking with the religious heads of this country in order to convince them to obtain whatever they wanted, or whatever they criticized, through talks, through consultation. [I urged them] to remember that they were Iranians and not to put the country in danger. That was my mistake. I'm sorry I didn't know what kind of people they were and that I was sincere and they were not."

[After his talk on the radio], everybody said, "Poor Pakravan. He made a mistake so he came and [apologized]." It wasn't that at all. What he said was, "They were not worth my time—not worth wasting my time to try to persuade them not to act that way."

HL: Why did he make this radio broadcast? It's unusual for the head of the security agency to do that.

FP: I know it's unusual. Because he was truthful, he was sincere and honest. His opinion was that first of all, as often as possible, you must tell the truth to the population of a country, because you must have some respect for them as adults, not as stupid idiots who don't understand anything except repression. Then he wanted to show to the people, to the population who had followed these people, that these religious [leaders], these mullahs, were not sincere. That whatever they had promised to him—because they had made promises: "Yes, General. You are absolutely right. We'll do exactly. We admire you. We respect you." He wanted to show them, so that they wouldn't follow. He wanted to tell the people, "You were duped by these people. They didn't tell you the truth. They didn't mind you being killed. They put your children in front of their processions. If the army had not received orders not to shoot, your small children aged from seven to twelve would have been killed." That was what he meant: that you have been duped by these people. "If they didn't want—if they refused to accept what I told them, what I asked them to do, they should have said no. They should have stood their ground."

Another thing my husband hated was lack of courage. One day I remember there were some people close to the shah who wanted to [involve] him in some hanky-panky. When they saw it was not so good, they begged a friend, a common friend, to meet Hassan, my husband, and to discuss the thing. They started, "You know, *timsar* [تیمسار, general], we didn't really want to do that. We didn't want to make a revolution." My husband looked at them. He said, "You know, you nauseate me." They were very surprised, because they were important people. I was there. He said, "You know, you nauseate me, because you want to subvert this country. But the moment you see that your safety might be in danger, you crawl." He said, "You don't have the courage." He said, "At least have the courage of your opinions and your actions. Be a man." He was disgusted by people who, you know, would like to do something and then when they saw that you stood your ground, they crawl.

Anyway, that was that. Now here I'm not very clear exactly on the time, because I was working, you know. I was working at the time myself. I always worked in Iran. So, I wasn't, how shall I say, I didn't have the same interest. I was interested, I won't say that, but I wasn't exactly politically minded, because as is the case for many royalists—people who think not particularly [of] this shah or another shah, but the idea of [monarchy] in a country—the regime of royalty prevents you from being [pulled] from left or right or middle or anything. You just want the regime to be there. Of course you want to improve it. You want to see it. You want to see it improved. You don't want things to stay exactly as they are. But you are not politically minded as in Europe or America.

Anyway, so I will sum up. Khomeini was arrested and taken into a villa, because the [security] organization had several villas where they received foreign guests like CENTO, or conferences and things like that.

And another thing which is interesting is that during the time of my husband, nobody ever said "SAVAK," except inside [the organization], you know, the people who worked there, I guess for [brevity], said "SAVAK." Outside it was always "Information and Security Organization." I never heard the word SAVAK. I remember making fun of them. I said, "It's ridiculous. SAVAK sounds like an Armenian first name." And I think there are Armenians called Savak. I said, "Why? I don't like [it]." Anyway, Khomeini was put in this villa, and I went back to Tehran.

Ayatollah Khomeini Under Detention

When we were in India, I had taken an orderly with me so that he would speak Persian with my children. During this time, I trained him as a butler and a cook. He was a very good butler. When we returned to Tehran and the Security Organization established a club, where receptions and conferences were held, we transferred him to the club. In the summer of 1978 [1357], my husband and this servant told me a few things.

The orderly told me that [during his detention in 1963/1342][31] Khomeini was in this villa and he had served him. He said, "I was told to pretend not to know that he was Khomeini." So I asked [the orderly] how it was. He said, "Well, [Ayatollah Khomeini] was very courteous, very nice.

---

[31] On 2 August 1963 (11 Mordad 1342), General Pakravan visited Ayatollah Khomeini in prison and told him that he was free to leave the detention center. The ayatollah was then moved and placed under house arrest in the Davoudieh district of Tehran. Ayatollah Hassan Ghomi and Ayatollah Bahaeddin Mahallati were soon taken to the same house, that of Haj Roghani, a bazaar merchant.

Every morning when I came, I would greet him, and he would greet me very nicely, and would say, 'What's new in town?' One day there was some unrest in the city, so I told him about it. He asked, 'Why?' I said, because Ayatollah Khomeini has distributed some tracts. And he [Khomeini] said in a very nice way, 'Can you give me a copy of this tract?' I said, 'Yes sir.' I rushed and brought it. He [Khomeini] really shook his head and said, 'I never wrote that!' I said, 'Oh, you are the ayatollah?' He said, 'Yes, my child. I am the ayatollah.'" That is what this ex-servant of mine told me.

My husband told me, "You know, I had lunch every week with the ayatollah." I said, "Yes. I knew that but you never told me what was the atmosphere of these meetings." He said, "Very good. Very cordial. Very friendly. The ayatollah used to say in this very flowery Eastern way, '*Timsar*, I count the days until we reach the day of our luncheon.'" I asked, "How was he?" My husband said, "He was very handsome. And I'm sure he's not as old as they say. I'll tell you why. He was very handsome. He had extraordinary presence, a power of seduction. He had a great charisma." (You know, charismatic is a word that is used very often now — charisma and all that — but actually in the Christian religion it's applied only to the holy spirit, because charisma means presents and also gifts. Okay?)

I asked my husband, "What was the subject of your conversation [with the ayatollah]? What did you talk about?" He said, "Well, about religion, about philosophy, about history."

I said, "Is he a very learned man?" He said, "Well, his religion, I cannot say, because I'm not a religious person. I suppose he is, because he is a specialist. But his ignorance in history and philosophy is something unbelievable." (You know, the man who said America has oppressed Iran for the last twenty-five centuries.) My husband said, "He's very, very, very ignorant." I said, "But what struck you in him? What did you find was the most striking aspect of his temperament or his character?" He said, "His ambition." I said, "Ambition? What do you mean ambition? What kind of ambition, political, religious?" He said, "I couldn't find out, because he's very secretive." Then he said, "You know, it made my hair stand on end. It was frightening."

HL: This meeting occurred in 1963 [1342]?

FP: Yes. He said, "It was frightening." And after that, well, I know that Khomeini was sent into exile.

HL: When did he tell you all of this?

Saving the Life of Ayatollah Khomeini

FP: In 1978 [1357] he started to tell me several things about his job which he had never told [before]. And you know that one of the adverse [items of] propaganda [that was being spread at the time] was that Khomeini had been rolled into a carpet, thrown into a sack, a bag, and taken to prison. It's not true. [The year] 1978 [1357] was a time when everybody believed every lie, even the burning of Cinema Rex.[32]

But at that time I said, "So, darling, he wasn't rolled into a carpet and taken?" He said, "Nonsense. We asked the Turks to be kind enough to accept him." And he said, "We gave him the red-carpet treatment. Then from there he wrote a very, very respectful letter to the shah"—this is a well-known fact—"[saying] 'allow me to go to Najaf, I want to study.'"

Now here is something I've learned recently from someone I can trust absolutely: well, everybody knows that my husband saved him. Khomeini was condemned to death. You know that?

HL: I had heard. I didn't know it for a fact.

FP: All right. He was condemned to death and my husband was very, very upset by that. He said he knew that, after all, the population of the country is not its elite. It's the real people. These are not very literate. They are simple. They are full of superstition. And even though most of the Iranians have no respect for the mullahs, they still have [respect] for what they represent. So he tried to convince the shah: "Please commute this." The shah said, "No. No. No." And my husband insisted. The shah said, "All right. But how?" After all, contrary to what people think, the shah wasn't a despot. He said, "After all, he was condemned by a tribunal. I cannot go over the [head of the] tribunal. Find a way, a legal way."

---

[32] On 19 August 1978 (28 Mordad 1357), 377 people were killed while watching a movie in the Rex Theater in Abadan. A fire had been set and the doors locked. Initially the SAVAK was blamed. However, further investigation pointed to other culprits.

My husband was on very good terms with Shariatmadari. So he went to see Shariatmadari and said, "Please, do something." And Shariatmadari said, "You know the only way is to make him an Ayatollah." So, they made a religious decree which is called *fatwa* [فتوى, decree], to make him Ayatollah—which he wasn't. And this was taken by my husband and Seyyed Jalal Tehrani[33] to the shah. And Seyyed Jalal Tehrani said afterwards, "It was the only time I kissed the shah's hand, so much I begged him."

And the shah said, "All right. And then what are your plans for him? You're not going to let him continue what he wants to do?" My husband said, "No. He should be sent to a far-away village, small village, where we can control his movements and control the people who go to see him, and after a while he'll be forgotten." He gave the example of another—Ayatollah Ghomi or something like that—who at one time wanted to make trouble and was exiled inside the country. This is very important.

[At that time] Amir-Asadollah Alam was prime minister. He said, "No. Let's send him away [to Turkey]." And somehow he convinced the shah. And my husband said to the shah,

---

[33] Seyyed Jalaleddin Tehrani, minister of state and assistant to the prime minister for parliamentary affairs (1947/1326), minister of state (1949–50/1328), minister of post and telegraph (1950/1328–29), appointed to the Second and Third Senate☐from Tabriz and the Fourth Senate from Tehran, and chairman of the Regency Council (1979/1357). He died in Paris in 1987/1366.

"You know, you're giving him the means. You give him an international platform." The shah said, "No. No. I think he promises that he will keep quiet." Of course, the rumor is that [Sheikh Sadegh] Khalkhali was sent [to Turkey] as a mullah, because there were many mullahs in the pay of the [Security Organization]. Apparently he was sent there too, but I don't believe it. Anyway, Khomeini was sent to Turkey.

[During] the summer of 1978 [1357], I asked my husband how he came to know Khomeini. [At that time] my husband had a position in the Ministry of Court. He came one day very thoughtful and a bit sarcastic. I said, "What's the matter?" He replied, "You know, I had a visitor today." (That was in 1978 [1357].) "And who was he?" I asked. He said, "A friend of Khomeini, who said, 'Please, *timsar*, go to Paris. Talk to *ayatollah ozma* [آیت الله عظما], the grand ayatollah]. You are the only one he would listen to.'" My husband [told the visitor], "You're mistaken. He will listen to nobody." The visitor had [responded],"Then let me go," because at the time Azhari[34] [had declared that] nobody should go. "Get me permission to go and get me a message from His Majesty for the ayatollah."

My husband had said, "I cannot do that." It was the time when they had made a horrible *montage* of the queen in the most insulting, in the most obscene way. [My husband had told his visitor], "You are a Muslim. You know that the wife

---

[34] General Gholam-Reza Azhari, chief of Supreme Commander's Staff (1971–78/1350–57) and prime minister (1978–79/1357).

of a Muslim is sacred for him. Nobody has the right to say anything. Do you think after the wife of the shah, the mother of his children, has been publicly insulted, and been insulted night and day, he will give a message of friendship to the ayatollah? You're greatly mistaken, but I can grant you permission to go." So he went, but wasn't received there [in Paris]. From what I hear he was executed [after the revolution]. That was Haj Roghani.[35] And my husband said [to me], "It's through him that I met Khomeini."

Before June 1963 [Khordad 1342], at the time he started, you know, in some very insidious way to subvert people, I was very mad. I was very annoyed, because they [the government] had big projects, you know. They really wanted to execute these big projects instead of having to deal with a few mad mullahs. And so Haj Roghani came [to see my husband]. Haj Roghani was a very peaceful man. He was terribly upset by fighting and unpleasantness. He was always trying to bring people together so that they would explain, talk to each other, and all that. So he came to my husband—that was in 1960, end of 1960 [1339]—[and said], "Let me take you to the ayatollah, to Imam, to Mr. Khomeini." (I don't want to use that name.) "He's very good. He's very intelligent. You'll like him." And this Haj Roghani was a merchant, a bazaar merchant

---

[35] Haj Roghani was a bazaar merchant in whose house Ayatollah Khomeini resided for several months in 1963/1342 when he was under house arrest [FP].

of Qom. Later he came to Tehran.

So my husband said, "Okay." He went all the way to Qom which is about 120 kilometers [south of Tehran]. He told me, "We went there. [Ayatollah Khomeini] came. He explained his position, and I explained mine. He stood by his position and I stood by my position. There was no point of meeting, because what he was saying was ridiculous. They had [based] all their propaganda on the [grounds] that the religious movement would be [suppressed] by the government, and that the government did [not] want to please the peasants who cultivated the land, but wanted to grab everything for itself. Also women would be turned into soldiers. The girls would be turned into soldiers, and naturally all the classic morality of the Persian girl would disappear, and Iran would become a country of completely immoral people." Unfortunately they [the government] did that in the end. Not the way he [Ayatollah Khomeini] said, but they had these [mixed police] units.

So [after June 1963/Khordad 1342] the page was turned and life went on. Everything was calm again. Don't forget that we had these [kinds of] upheavals and uprisings all the time. My sister [who] is married to an American, gave me letters I [had written] her in the 1940s [1320s], [indicating] that we always had uprisings and killings and martial law. [Iran] is a very, very violent country, contrary to what people say.

Assassination of Prime Minister Hassan-Ali Mansour

In January of 1965 [Bahman 1343], my husband was on a mission to Kurdistan. There was some unrest. I was personally [at the office of] Mr. Pahlbod,[36] the minister of fine arts. We [were to have] a meeting. For some reason, [Mr. Pahlbod] never appeared. We asked the head of his staff, "Where is His Excellency?" He [the head of his staff] received a secret telephone call [and] became pale and said, "Well, His Excellency will not be able to come." The Ministry of Fine Arts is quite close to the Majles, on the Parliament Square in Tehran.

[I left the ministry and headed for my office.] I was working at the National Tourist Organization, as the head of research and planning. When I reached my office, my husband telephoned me. No. No. My husband didn't telephone me. Everybody, the whole office was [pause]. "What's happened?" I asked. "They've killed Mansour, Hassan-Ali Mansour," I was told. He was coming from the Parliament and somebody killed him. Ten bullets, I think it was. I was horrified. "My God. We're going to have a revolution," I thought. "My husband is not here." I rushed to my house. I [told] the driver to go and fetch the children and [thought] let's go into our house and be safe there.

We went to the hospital. As you know, Mansour didn't die

---

[36] Mehrdad Pahlbod, assistant to Prime Minister Mansour and director of culture and arts (1964/1343), and minister of culture and arts (1964–78/1343–57).

Memoirs of Fatemeh Pakravan

immediately; he was wounded. They kept him alive for seven days. However, even if he had been cured, he would have been like a vegetable. They brought Professor Sicard, whom I met [in Paris later] when my husband was ambassador. He became a kind of friend. He never, never, never, never said what exactly happened, [or] what was his diagnosis.

And Madam Hassan-Ali Mansour, Farideh, when she saw my husband, went into his arms and cried and said [pause]. I don't know what she said. But when Nassiri, head of the police, came, she said, "I don't want to see this man. It's all his fault." She might have accused my husband of not having been vigilant, because it was also part of his job to know the situation.

Pakravan Becomes Minister of Information

Anyway, Mansour died. Hoveida became prime minister, and my husband became minister of information. [Initially it was] very widely rumored that he would have two jobs. I said, "It's ridiculous. You cannot be minister of information and also head of the Security Organization. It doesn't go together."

HL: So, for a while he had both jobs?

FP: No. No. Not at all. The public rumor had it, because you know, they admired my husband, even the public. You know, when he became head of the so-called SAVAK, they said, «امام حسین رئیس ساواک شده» [Imam Hossein[37] has become

---
[37] Imam Hossein, son of Hazrat-e Ali, the third imam of the Shiites, was referred to as *mazlum* [مظلوم, wronged].

chief of SAVAK]. He was greatly admired. And he always used to say, "No. No. No. If people knew me, they would never admire me"—because he had this sense of humor.

HL: Why did he leave the Security Organization? What happened?

FP: What happened? I can only tell you this. In my opinion, the shah thought, the shah didn't [pause]. What Hoveida told me—I'll tell you exactly what Hoveida said. I knew Hoveida [from when] we were all young, and he used to say *tu* to me in French. We always spoke French together. And he said, "Do you know I made Hassan minister of information?" I said, "Really?" He said, "Yes. When the shah called me for consultation and asked me whom I would choose for my government, suddenly he asked, 'And the minister of information? Without thinking I said, 'Pakravan.'" I asked him, "What happened?" Hoveida replied, "Well, the shah was a bit thoughtful. He said, 'Pakravan? Well, I want him to decide himself. Please ask him.'" And Hoveida said, "I asked Hassan. Hassan said, 'Oh, thank God! I'm finished with this security.'" But I cannot tell you if it's absolutely true.

HL: But your husband didn't say anything to you at the time when he [interrupted]?

FP: No. No. He said Hoveida asked him to become the minister of information and he was glad in a way. He thought that perhaps through the radio and television (at the time everything was [under the control of] the Ministry of

Information) [he could tell] the truth to the people. [And] through organizing the information in a really proper way, he'd somehow educate public opinion in Iran.

I remember one of the first things he asked me. He said, "Find me everything you can in French literature about calumny and slander. I want this to be repeated every day. And the motto is: 'Slander, slander people. Even if it's proved not true, something remains.'" You know, you tell something bad about a person, even if it's proven [to be false], it remains.

Then he had these *tafsir-e siyasi* [تفسیر سیاسی] — these [political] commentaries on foreign and domestic news. Hossein Loghman-Adham, chief of protocol at the court, said, "You know, it's funny. At 2:30 [P.M.], no matter who is there at the court, who has finished his lunch or not, everybody rushes to listen to [the political commentary on the radio]."

Shah's Reaction to Pakravan's Execution

HL: So his transfer from the Security Organization was not indicative of a falling out or disagreement with the shah?

FP: No. No. No. Absolutely not. You know, my daughter, my eldest daughter, saw the shah a week before he died. And my sister saw him in hospital in America when [the shah] had already left the country. My sister is very direct. She said, "Your Majesty, why didn't you take my brother-in-law [out of Iran] with you?" (The shah didn't take anybody, and my husband wouldn't go. I'll tell you that. This is personal, but never mind.)

And [my sister asked the shah], "Did you have some grudge against him, because he didn't let the Iranian justice execute Khomeini [in 1963/1342]?" And she said that [the shah] became pale and said, "How can you say a thing like this? I liked and admired [him]." And the queen [who] was there said, "You know, of all the things that happened to us since we left Iran," (because they knew he was killed and all that) "the thing that nearly drove us mad was the execution of General Pakravan. This is the thing that really finished us."

And then again my daughter saw [the shah], a week, just a week, before he died in Cairo. [She] also heard the testimony of Henri Bonnier. He is the literary director of Albin Michel, the publishing house that published the shah's memoir.[38] He used to follow [the shah] everywhere. He went to Mexico, to Panama, to San Antonio in Texas, to Cairo, wherever the shah was, because they were trying to bring all the pages to start the book as fast as possible. He swore that the shah wrote [the book] himself.

He [Henri Bonnier] said, "You know, we were discussing, we were talking. Naturally there [were many topics] he was always going back to. He said I asked him, "Your Majesty, you've reigned since 1941 [1320]. You mean to say that among all these people [that worked for you] there was nobody [who was a] friend of yours? Nobody that you could trust? Nobody

---

[38] For the English language version of this book see Mohammad Reza Pahlavi, *The Shah's Story* (London: Michael Joseph, 1980).

that you could listen to?" And then [Henri Bonnier] said [the shah] became very thoughtful and said, "Yes. There was a wonderful person—a man—who always told me the truth: a man who was devoted to me, a man who was never lowly and crawling, but I didn't understand it at the time. And that was Pakravan."

I was very touched by this testimony, and the fact that he admitted that he didn't understand [it earlier]. In the last few months before [the shah] left Iran, he was pleading with my husband like that. I asked my husband. I said, "But why?" He said, "You know, my presence reassured him, perhaps because as young men we started to work together. Perhaps he remembers a few things. Anyway, when I go [to the court], he morally clings to me as if I was a boy who gives him some feeling of security." It was very pathetic.

Second Session: 7 March 1983 (16 Esfand 1361)

Her Own Background

HL: Mrs. Pakravan, now that we have more time, I want to ask you to give a little bit of a background about yourself and your own family, and then about your own education and work at the Najmiyeh Hospital.

FP: Well, my father and mother met in Tiflis in the middle of the [Russian] revolution. [After] my father married my mother, [he] brought her back to Iran. Unfortunately, after a while they didn't [get along] together, and in 1928 [1307] my father convinced my mother to let my sister and me go to Paris with him where he had settled. He wanted to give—he believed very much in the French education and he loved France very, very much.

HL: Were they both Iranian?

FP: No. My mother was half Polish and half Russian. So we reached Paris after a very long journey, because we stopped everywhere. We reached Paris in January of 1929 [1307] and were put in a convent to be educated here [Paris] at Pension Saint Honoré.

[As] you know, in 1937 [1316] Reza Shah abolished the *chador* [چادر, veil] for women.[39] He wanted them to really

---

[39] On 8 January 1936 (17 Dey 1314) use of the veil was outlawed in Iran.

participate in life. He also more or less obliged them to wear a hat—starting with his own family: the queen and his daughters, and the wives of all the ministers, members of government, and high officials of his administration.

Although my father wasn't a fanatical Muslim, he was very much against all that, but somehow there were things that he was attached to. So, he said, "You will study to be a midwife, because I'm sure that despite all the regulation, Iranian women will not agree to go to a male doctor to have their babies."

So, I went to this school which I didn't like at all, and when I went back to Iran, I didn't know Persian very well. That's why many people think I'm French, because my natural language is French. I was quite a small child when I came [to France].

[When I] finished my studies, my father didn't want me to go to Iran. He said, "You know, you've been completely brought up like a French girl. You will not be happy in Iran. You don't know Iranians very well." I said, "No, [but] I want to go." He said, "Okay. You go. But I know that you will not be able to live there. But you must bear it for two years. After two years, if it's really unbearable, then you can come back to France."

In the meantime, there was the war and I met my husband in the summer of 1940 [1319]. We were married in February of 1941 [1319].

HL: Did you meet in Tehran?

FP: Yes. We met in Tehran. And very naturally, like every

woman, I think that it was [under] very romantic circumstances. I think all marriages, more or less, are in romantic circumstances. When I went back to Iran, I wanted very much to work. My idea was to work in a public hospital. Of course, I was full of ideals and I thought we have to serve—you know, things you have when you are very, very young. But there was no Ministry of Health at the time in Iran. There was a general directorate of hygiene, and I was offered a very, very minor job with a really ridiculous salary.

Working at the Najmiyeh Hospital

In the meantime, a friend of my father, Dr. Javad Ashtiani,[40] fetched me and took me to [meet] Dr. Gholam-Hossein Mossadegh at the Najmiyeh Hospital. They had a Swiss director, and she had left suddenly. So, Dr. Ashtiani introduced me to Dr. Mossadegh who immediately gave me the job. Because the former director was always addressed as "Mademoiselle," I became "Mademoiselle" in my turn. And everybody spoke French to me, because I didn't know enough Persian. And that's how the idea came about that I am either French or Armenian. Even people who know me very well, are sometimes

---

[40] Dr. Javad Ashtiani, son of Haj Hashem (cleric and Majles deputy), received his medical education in Paris. Upon return to Iran, his positions included dean of the Medical School, Tehran University; Fifteenth Majles deputy from Tehran (1947–49/1326–28), and minister of health (1961/1339–40). He was appointed to the Fourth Senate☐from Shiraz, and elected to the Fifth through the Seventh Senate from Tehran.

surprised to find that I am actually Iranian.

Anyway, I worked there until my marriage. My husband was entirely educated abroad. His mother was half French and half Iranian. Among his ancestors he had two French great-grandmothers, and an Austrian great-great grandfather, named Stephan von Herzfeld, who was an officer and is now in all the books about Mexico. He was a great friend of Maximilian and [joined him] when Maximilian was supposed to become the emperor of Mexico. This [Austrian] ancestor of my husband became the Marquis of Cuernavaca, [the city] in Mexico where the shah [resided for a while during his exile.]

Anyway, my husband suddenly became very, very Eastern and decided that his wife must not work, that he must provide for her. But, he couldn't provide for me, because he was a young captain and the army officers were very, very underpaid. So, we had to live with my mother-in-law, [Emineh Pakravan], who was a professor at the University of Tehran. She was also a writer in French.

In France they have a prize which is given to foreign authors who write directly in French. It's called the Prix Rivarol. It's a very famous prize and she got that for a very, very good book. By the way, I tried to have her books published in America, but apparently they were not interested.

And so I stopped working and had my first child, but we couldn't manage, because Tehran entered the war.[41] Don't forget

---

[41] Iran was invaded by the Anglo-Soviet forces on 25 August

that the country was occupied by the Russians, the British with their colonial armies—that means the Gurkhas,[42] the Indians, the Sikhs,[43] and what they call Anzac—that's [a soldier from] New Zealand or Australia—and later by Americans. So life became very, very difficult in Tehran. The Allies had arrested and put into camps all those they suspected of sympathy with the Germans.

There was a shortage of practically everything, and so naturally the price of living shot up. Nobody could afford to live unless they were very, very rich. It's difficult to visualize the Tehran of that time. I mean, there [were] only two lines of buses and practically no cars. You knew exactly who had a car—the court, a few ministers, and a few rich people.□ So I went back to work, but this time at the hospital of the National Bank [*Bank-e Melli-e Iran*, بانك ملى ايران] with Dr. Raji.[44]

It had just been inaugurated and I worked there for a while until in 1943 or 1944 [1322 or 1323]. There was some trouble with my replacement at the Najmiyeh Hospital. And Dr. [Mohammad] Mossadegh, that is the "father" of the famous

---

1941 (3 Shahrivar 1320).

[42] Soldiers from Nepal serving in the British army.

[43] Adherents of a monotheistic religion of India founded about 1500 by a Hindu under Islamic influence and marked by rejection of idolatry and caste.

[44] Dr. Abdolhossein Raji, son of Abdolhamid Ala al-Hokama, received his university education in medicine in Paris. He held various posts including deputy to the Fifteenth, Sixteenth, and Nineteenth Majles from Khorramshahr, and was minister of health (1957–60/1336–38).

oil nationalization, insisted that I should come back. So I went back there, but told him that I would not stay for ever and ever, because my father was in Paris. I had no news from him during all the time of the war, except through the Vatican and the Red Cross. [I insisted that] the moment peace was around the corner, I wanted to go back to France. They said, "Okay. Peace is not around the corner [now]."☐

Anyway, in 1945 [1324] my father came to Tehran, and didn't like it at all. He went back [to Paris] and waited for us.

Fathollah Pakravan

After a while when the war was finished, my father-in-law was appointed as ambassador to Italy.

HL: Your father-in-law being?

FP: The father of my husband.

HL: Yes.

FP: My father-in-law was a very close—how shall I say—associate of Reza Shah. Reza Shah trusted him and liked him very much. During the time of Reza Shah, he had been governor-general of Khorasan. He was practically the only person who resisted the Russians, the only official who resisted the Russians. It's a famous story. When the Russians invaded Iran in 1941 [1320]—and naturally they had their [headquarters] in Mashhad—suddenly there was absolutely a shortage of everything. My father-in-law was a very proud and very—how shall I say—strong-willed man. He sat himself beside the drivers of trucks, and went and took out the flour wherever it was, and obliged the bakers to bake bread. He himself went to distribute [the bread].

When the commanding officer of the Russian forces asked him to come [and pay him a visit], he refused.[45] He sent a message saying, "You say that you've come to Iran as our ally. If you're our ally, you must respect those who represent the central government of my country. So it's up to you to come and call on me." And the [Russian officer] did.☐ Anyway, he [my father-in-law] was arrested.[46]

We went through a period of terrible trouble after the shah abdicated.[47] This was a time of revenge and accusation. Anybody close to Reza Shah was arrested. Of course, they couldn't find anything, so they [released] him [my father-in-law].

After a while they wanted to make him governor of Azerbaijan which he refused, because it was occupied by the Russians. They wanted to make him governor of Khorasan again. He refused. He said he had done so much for Khorasan and the Khorasanis were so ungrateful. By the way, later on, they came to beg him to come back, but he refused. They

---

[45] Mohammad-Ebrahim Amirteymour Kalali confirms and praises this resistance. See *Memoirs of Mohammad-Ebrahim Amirteymour Kalali* (Cambridge, Mass.: Harvard Center for Middle Eastern Studies, 1997), p. 254.

[46] In 1942/1321 he was arrested for his alleged role in the execution of governor-general Mohammad-Vali Assadi on 21 December 1935 (29 Azar 1314). Ibid.

[47] Reza Shah abdicated on 16 September 1941 (25 Shahrivar 1320).

wanted to make him prime minister; he refused also. I asked him why. He said, "Because they don't really want me to be [of] service to the country. They just want to finish me. It's not the [right] time [for me] to be prime minister. There is somebody else and other forces arranged for here." Anyway, they asked him what he wanted to be. And he said, well, he wanted to finish [his] career in Rome, so he went there [as ambassador].

Years at Iranian Airways

So, in 1947 [1326] I took my two daughters by plane to Rome where I stayed with my father-in-law for a while. Then [we went] by train to Paris. I stayed eight months in France and then I went back to Iran. At that time I decided that I was completely fed up with working in a hospital. I couldn't stand to see people ill and dying. I couldn't. So I decided to change completely my aim in life. I was hired by the Iranian Airways which was a private company belonging to the Afshars and Gholam-Hossein Ebtehaj and all these people. I became secretary—what they call in French *secrétaire de direction*. And little by little, you know, because of my English and French, I became a jack of all trades.

I stayed there until we went to Pakistan the first time in the summer of 1949 [1328], and back again in May 1950 [1329], as I told you. Then they took me back to my job. And they did that several times, and every time they increased my salary. So I said, "It's a good point—I'll go away for a few months, when I come back you increase my salary!" Anyway, the last time was in 1954 [1333] when we left for India, and when I came back, I didn't go to that job. I just worked in welfare, you know.

Then I taught French at the Institute for Foreign Languages which is part of Tehran University. At the same time, I became the director of RSPA, the Society for the Protection of Animals. I was also practically all my life a member of the Persian Red Cross which was called the Red Lion and Sun Association [جمعیت شیر و خورشید سرخ ایران].

Doing Social Work

I remember that we started to establish a little society which we wanted to [keep] completely free from the royal family. [At that time] anybody who did any welfare [work] always tried to have a member of the royal family [on their board of directors]. This spoiled everything—not because of the royal family, but because it gave another meaning to the whole point.

So I asked a few friends of mine, teachers at the university, Ehsan Naraghi,[48] General Stodach,—what's his name?—he had been chief of staff of the air service. [With] several people like that, we decided that we must absolutely and very urgently do something about the people—what is now called the *lumpenproletariat*—that means this fringe of people who lived in the

---

[48] Ehsan Naraghi, sociologist and professor at Tehran University.

south of big cities, especially in Tehran. As I told you, [they all lived] in caverns [that were] dug up to make bricks. These people lived in the most incredible way.

It was exactly as if they didn't belong to the country. They had their own laws, their own regulations, and naturally their own traffic, child prostitution, organized beggary (I mean organized, because they made people appear blind or wounded, or have all kinds of disease which was all made-up), traffic in drugs, and of course a wonderful hiding place for all kinds of petty criminals. [It was] also a very good reservoir of people who had nothing to lose. That's the kind of people that Khomeini uses; and Mossadegh often used in a way also. This is the people among whom—the kind of Mafia we used to have in Iran, you know, *Shaban bimokh* [شعبان بی مخ], "the brainless Shaban," all these people who were big dealers in the wholesale markets of Tehran. Actually, they were real gangsters. They gave protection, you see. They also had the control of the [red-light district] of Tehran.

And these people, we thought at the time (it was in the late 1950s [1330s]), numbered about 14,000. And we knew that in a matter of ten years there would be ten times as many and so on and so on. And it would represent an immense danger for the country. And also my friends and I thought that it was really absolutely against every sense of justice and even welfare—not the welfare of these people, but the rest of the capital, the rest of the country, to allow this kind of cancerous society to grow, you see.

So we started with a little. They were called *zagheh neshin* [زاغـﮥ نشـین], people living in caves that was the area of, how shall I say, the "nest" people, because they were not living in houses. They had [hovels] that they somehow managed to organize for themselves. And those who were honest had the most fantastic jobs—incredible.

I remember visiting a family. They were only women—the mother with five girls living in a small room. They had an immense heap of thread completely knotted. I said, "What are you doing?" They said they were paid five rials (I don't know how much is five rials now) unraveling these very, very, very thin threads for hosiery factories to make stockings. Can you imagine the job? Unraveling wool is already difficult, but this very thin thread—this was the kind of job they had!

So we started [small]. I didn't believe in big things, you know. I always believed in the things that you start small. Then when there are strong roots, then you spread. So with my friends we agreed that we would take over a small area, which funnily enough, was in the middle of the city—at Behjatabad.

Now, Behjatabad had been a camp during the war, when the Allies were in Iran. During the war, the Russians made all kinds of promises to the Armenians, saying, "Go back to Armenia. Why do you stay here where you're not in your [own] country? You're Armenians. Go back there."

So they [the Armenians] rushed from all over the country

(mostly from Esfahan and the countryside of Esfahan, because there they were agriculturalists) to Tehran—from where they were supposed to be taken by the Russians to Armenia and they were stuck there. So the government with the help of the Armenian community (that was, after all, quite rich and prosperous) established these camps. They didn't know what to do with these people. They couldn't go back, because they had sold everything. And on top of that, they had lost face before those Armenians who refused to go. They didn't have anywhere to go and were completely stuck there.

Anyway, somehow they were resettled. Some of them actually went to Russia. The others were distributed in various Armenian communities, but the camp remained. And because life was so difficult in small cities of Iran and in the countryside, all these poor people came to Tehran with the hope of finding a job. They settled [in Behjatabad] in little hovels they built for themselves.

We had a very, very good plan to resettle these people. The principle was that with our help they should do it themselves. They should do everything themselves, because we didn't want to create mendicants and beggars. We wanted to give them their sense of dignity—that they had brought themselves up by their own efforts.

And we had the help of students from the university. We were very, very grateful. We wanted to use them, because we realized very soon that the university people, especially the students, were not taken seriously, you know. I'm not the one to make demagogy for youth, because I think that this is the time for effort and we must not flatter the young. We must show them the way in a sincere way.

So these people [students] had nothing. There was no kind of amusement in Tehran. No kind of incentive, you know. I remember, every time I talked to a young person, my first question was, "Do you read?" And they said, "No. What is reading?" They just looked through papers. Nobody explained to them that it's not enough to go to university—that beside university, you have to work by yourself. You must use what you learn at the university as the guideline to improve your mind, and you improve your mind by reading, by reflecting, by talking to people who have something to give you. That was something entirely new, and sometimes they didn't trust people who told them these things. So we thought we'd ask them to come and participate in this kind of a job—instead of always criticizing—and let them put their hand into the mud and try to clean it.

That was very well, except that naturally we fell into bureaucracy. The shah somehow learned about [our efforts] and he said, "Very good. Give me some reports." We made a small report. We said we didn't want anybody's help. Land surrounding Behjatabad, which was in the middle of the city and adjacent to the elegant part of the city, was very expensive. The poor owners of this land had been promised many times that something would be done: they would be [compensated for their occupied land].

Ahmad Nafisi was the vice mayor [at the time]. He showed us very good land that was already prepared with electricity, water, and we were going to settle [these people] there. So, we were very happy. "We don't want any money," [we told the landowners]. "We ask each of you to give us building materials in proportion to your piece of land and have your lawyers ensure that [the new settlement] will not be built on your land."

Well, it's a long story. It didn't come to anything, because they wanted us to become part of this enormous thing, *ordu-ye kar* [اردوی کار, work camp]. It was the so-called resettlement of beggars. That was a big plan. Anyway, this went to the dogs and I was busy with other things. I worked very hard at it, but we didn't [pause]. Somehow I suppose people—those who were in responsible positions—didn't like [that]. Perhaps didn't want that.

National Tourist Organization

While in India [1954–57/1333–36], I had been very impressed by the handiworks of the various states of Delhi and everywhere. And I'd been impressed by the fact that the Indians were intelligent enough to understand that handiwork was beautiful, but it was always repetitive. So they brought artists from abroad, mostly from France, to use the methods of this craft, but to adapt it to the taste of the Europeans—the Westerners who were the best customers for that kind of thing.

So I came back to Iran and I wanted very much to start this handicraft in Iran. At the time, Asadollah Alam was the head of the Pahlavi Foundation. Here I must say that he was very, very well disposed towards my husband's family, because they were also from Birjand, south of Khorasan, and they had established somehow the best of relationships with my father-in-law.

So Asadollah Alam received me, and said, "How wonderful. We'll start it from the Pahlavi Foundation." We had to be attached [to the Foundation]. I couldn't start that [operation myself]. I never had any money. I didn't have the personal means. We had to start somewhere.

I started to gather friends and all that, when suddenly [Mr. Alam] said that the government had decided to revive the tourist organization founded by Reza Shah as the Iran Tour Company.[49] Tourism in Iran which was half-asleep [was] attached to the Ministry of Roads. Amir-Asadollah Alam told me that they wanted to establish a new organization for tourism, and that the [new] organization would work through a high council (we like high council of this and that very much in Iran) of tourism and also through committees. [He also told me that] I would become the secretary-general of the high

---

[49] In all probability this event occurred at the outset of Asadollah Alam's premiership, 19 July 1962 (28 Tir 1341).

council and also in charge of all committees, including the one for handicraft.

So we started very modestly with Mehdi Sheibani[50] as head of the [National Tourist Organization]. At the time there was no parliament in Iran.[51] Shortly after that, Asadollah Alam became prime minister and the government governed by decree. And so we were established with a decree. That was a very fascinating job. I liked it very much until the government changed again.

Hassan-Ali Mansour became prime minister and he kicked out everybody except me.[52] He had a new head of [tourist] organization who reorganized everything. My colleagues and I were put aside a little bit, because the new head of the organization, Ghassem Rezai, was convinced that my little part of this organization was a kind of branch of the Security Organization. And I am very, very direct. I told him one day, "You know, my husband doesn't need me. I'm sure that he has agents in your organization. I don't know them. I'm working [here] because I like this job. That's all." So, we established a very good relationship after that.

---

[50] Mehdi Sheibani was appointed deputy prime minister and director of tourist affairs on 15 December 1962 (24 Azar 1341) by Prime Minister Alam.

[51] The Twentieth Majles was dissolved by the shah on 9 May 1961 (19 Ordibehesht 1340). The Twenty-first Majles was inaugurated on 6 October 1963 (14 Mehr 1342).

[52] Hassan-Ali Mansour formed his cabinet on 9 March 1964 (19 Esfand 1342).

After some trial and error—[although Mr. Rezai] did not completely cancel the high council—he [no longer] used [it], but he [appointed] me head of planning and development of tourism, *modir-e tarh-ha va barressi-ha* [مدیر طرح‌ها و بررسی‌ها]. [Then, Mr. Rezai] made the mistake of going to the other extreme. I became his *ma'lumat* [معلومات], his thinking brains, his right-hand man.

HL: So you began to work together?

FP: So we started. It was a very fascinating job. I liked it very much. I even went to the First United Nations Conference on Tourism which took place in Rome in September of 1964 [1343]—I think. I don't know. Yes, in 1963 [1342].

When I came back, Sheibani was still the head.[53] He said, "Go and see the shah." I must say that the thing I was [most] proud [of] was the reorganization of the Golestan Palace. Of course I didn't achieve it, but that was our plan with Mohsen Foroughi[54] and other people.

And so I went to see the shah. The interesting thing is that [it was] my only public audience [with him]. I knew the shah, of course. I met him very often and all that. What was interesting [was that] first of all I saw how the shah could be courteous

---

[53] Ghassem Rezai replaced Mehdi Sheibani as head of the National Tourist Organization on 7 March 1964 (17 Esfand 1342).

[54] Mohsen Foroughi, son of Mohammad-Ali (prime minister). University education in Paris, civil engineer and professor, Tehran University. Nineteenth Majles deputy from Tehran (resigned), appointed to the Fifth Senate☐ from Esfahan, Sixth and Seventh Senate from Tehran, and minister of culture and arts (1978/1357).

and attentive to what people said. He listened very carefully, and after I finished, he asked questions. He asked, "What is your greatest difficulty in this job?" I said, "Regulations." He said, "What do you mean?" I said, "Regulations in this country are not made to advance the affairs of the country but to paralyze [them]."

We discussed this point at length. Then he said, "What would you do if you were in charge? What would you do with the regulations?" I said, "I would take them to the middle of Meydan-e Sepah,[55] and burn them." He said, "Well, that's rather extreme. Isn't it?" Then he asked, "What was the most important conclusion of the United Nations Conference on Tourism?" I said, "As you know, the United Nations cannot impose anything; they can just suggest and advise. They [decided] that all of us must obtain from our respective governments the [pledge] that the Ministry of Information, wherever it exists, would never be mixed with tourism. They are two different activities."

And the shah said, "Why?" I said, "May I speak very [frankly]?" He said, "Yes. Do." I said, "Your Majesty, you know that the Ministry of Propaganda,[56] — now [called] the Ministry of Information, or whatever — [as indicated by] its

---

[55] Meydan-e Sepah, formerly known as Meydan-e Tupkhaneh, was located in the central section of Tehran.

[56] The Ministry of Information was formed out of the former Department of Propaganda in 1964/1342 by Prime Minister Hassan-Ali Mansour.

own name is a political instrument to enhance a country's facilities inside [and outside] the country. Because it is political, it can always exaggerate and say: 'The sky of Iran is the bluest. The water of Iran is the best. The fruits of Iran are unique,' and all that. But in tourism they cannot say that, because if a man comes by car [over our poor roads] and breaks his [shock absorbers] every other kilometer, or he doesn't find good roads, or he doesn't find hotels, or a place even to wash his hands, then we [are making] false propaganda. We must be truthful. We must give them good, precise information about the climate, what to wear, when to come, what kind of roads [to expect], how to travel, how to behave, etc., etc." [The shah] quite agreed, but eventually, as you know, they did that—they mixed the two [propaganda and tourism] together.

Ambassador to Pakistan (1966–68/1345–47)

Well, that was finished, because my husband was named ambassador to Pakistan and we went there. [While in Pakistan], Mr. Pahlbod[57] wanted me to be in charge of cultural affairs at the embassy. I tried to convince him that it was impossible; you couldn't have a diplomatic list with "General Pakravan, as ambassador [and] Mrs. Pakravan, as counselor for cultural affairs." [Mr. Pahlbod] said, "All right then. I'll name somebody [else], but you will be actually in charge."

When I went to Pakistan, I worked as head of cultural

---

[57] Mehrdad Pahlbod, minister of culture and arts.

affairs and that was very, very interesting. We gathered a lot of information [about] the progress or regression of the Persian language, [such as] where it was taught, etc., etc. And that was that. Now you ask me questions.

Second Term at the Najmiyeh Hospital

HL: I'm going to ask you about a number of historical figures, some of whom you may know well, some of whom you may not know personally. I will begin with Dr. Mossadegh. Did you ever meet him?

FP: Of course!

HL: What sort of an impression did you have of him?

FP: You know, I don't want to give you my impression now, because it's different from what I felt when I was a young girl. When I was put in charge of the hospital the first time, after a while his son said, "My father will come and inspect the hospital and talk to you." I said, "All right."

One day this very distinguished Iranian gentleman [came to the hospital]. [He was] very elegant because he didn't wear the kind of Mao Tse-tung clothes [he wore later]. He was wearing Western clothes. In his physical aspects, he reminded me of a French writer. He was really *grand seigneur*—very courteous, very, very nice, [and] spoke French beautifully and addressed me in French. He had sent flowers beforehand. He asked me many questions and encouraged me in my job and was very, very nice."

Then somehow, I became great friends with his son, [Doctor] Gholam-Hossein [Mossadegh] and [Mohammad Mossadegh's wife], Zia al-Saltaneh. So when [Mohammad Mossadegh] asked me to come back [to the Najmiyeh Hospital], I went to see him. [Najmiyeh] was the most important private hospital in Tehran. At the time, we never even mentioned the public hospitals, [because] they were so awful. [During my meeting with Dr. Mossadegh, I told him], "You know, Dr. Mossadegh, the first time I worked here, I was quite a young girl. I didn't know anything. I came straight from school to run a hospital. But since then, I have [developed] my [own] ideas of how to run a hospital. I want you to please accept that—within the confines of the hospital—I am the absolute master. Doctors, the surgeons, the nurses, [and] absolutely the visitors must accept the rules I'm going to establish for this hospital." He said, "All right. Do that."

So the first thing I did was to establish visiting hours, because we could never do anything for the patients. People used to come in the hospital with their carpets, their charcoal stoves or kerosene stoves—I mean all the family: children and grandchildren. They would spread their carpets and really [have a] picnic there, smoke cigarettes, speak aloud, come and go any time of day or night.

Another thing which I wanted to do was to give the nurses and the hospital staff a day off and more holidays [and also to have them wear] uniform. Little by little [I got] rid of the so-called practical nurses and [employed] trained nurses. [Unfortunately] we didn't have great sources; we had only the American School. Later on, two very, very good schools were established for training nurses.

Mossadegh, I must say, kept to his word. One time a general came at 11:00 at night. He wanted to visit his wife who had just had a baby. I said, no. The doorkeeper came and said, "He's making a scandal at the door." I said, "Let him." So I went to [the door] and talked to him. I said, "You cannot make such a noise in a hospital. Your wife is not the only patient here." He said, "You are a dog attached to this place. You are not a director. I'm going to have you kicked out of this place." I said, "Okay. Do that."

So the next day, he went to Mossadegh al-Saltaneh and complained, "Why is that girl—that woman [behaving this way]?" And [Mossadegh responded], "You know, I cannot [do] anything, because even if I went to the hospital, I [would] have to submit to the rules she has [set]." And so the [general] came [back] the next day with flowers and nylon stockings (which were very rare) and said, "I'm sorry." I said, "Look here. I'm going to speak very plainly to you. You know a patient—whether a surgery patient or a gynecology patient—has some natural needs in daytime. How can they satisfy those if the room is always full of visitors?" Mossadegh was very, very good.

HL: Why was Mossadegh al-Saltaneh so involved in the

administration of the hospital?

FP: Because he was the head. The Najmiyeh Hospital was a foundation [established] by his mother, Najm al-Saltaneh, a very high [Qajar] princess and sister of Farmanfarma.[58] And [Mossadegh al-Saltaneh] was the head of the endowment—of *moqufeh* [موقوفه]. And people knew him. He was, after all, one of the great, important people of Iran. So [the general] thought if he went directly to him, he would immediately kick me out of the hospital.

HL: And what was the role of his son, Gholam-Hossein Khan?

FP: He was a surgeon and director of the hospital. He was the head of the medical part of the hospital. We had many other doctors. We had Dr. Moaven, Professor Adl,[59] Dr. [Jahangir] Vossoughi. All the best doctors used to come there.

---

[58] Abdolhossein Farmanfarma was the second son of Firouz Mirza Nosrat al-Dowleh. Born in 1858/1237, he inherited his father's title upon his death in 1885/1264. When his older brother died in 1892/1271, he acquired the title of Farmanfarma. He received military training in the Austrian army, and married Ezzat al-Saltaneh, daughter of Mozaffar al-Din Shah. His own sister, Hazrat-e Olya, was married to Mozaffar al-Din Shah. He was governor of Fars (1897–99/1276–78), exiled to Baghdad (1899–1903/1278–82), governor of Kermanshah (1903/1282), Second Majles deputy from Arak, minister of justice (1907/1285), governor of Azerbaijan (1908/1287–88), minister of the interior (1909/1288), minister of justice (1909/1288), minister of the interior (1910/1289), minister of war (1910–12/1289–90), minister of the interior (1915/1294), and prime minister (1915–16/1294).

[59] Yahya Adl, prominent surgeon, one of a small circle of men around the shah, appointed to the Second, Third, Fifth, Sixth, and Seventh Senate and elected to the Fourth Senate from Tehran.

One day Dr. Moaven, a brilliant surgeon, who had been put in prison by Reza Shah because he was friends with foreigners, which was forbidden, became a member of the parliament for Saleh, somewhere near Kermanshah.[60] I was still very naive at the time. I thought that political life in Iran was like Europe: that there were elections, and you had political parties, and members of such and such parties went to the parliament and decided on policy and things. So I asked him, "What is your party [affiliation]?" He laughed and said, "My pocket and Dr. Mossadegh." He brought out a little syringe for [injection out of his pocket, and explained], "You know, Dr. [Mohammad] Mossadegh is member of parliament and whenever somebody stands up to him or something doesn't please him, he faints." [Dr. Moaven], of course, didn't believe in this fainting. "So, I give him some injections to revive him."

Anyway, I wasn't very, very politically minded at the time. There was a big fight between Ghavam al-Saltaneh,[61] — who

---

[60] Dr. Hossein Moaven was elected to the Fourteenth Majles from the city of Kermanshah.

[61] Ahmad Ghavam (Ghavam al-Saltaneh), son of Mirza Ebrahim Motamed al-Saltaneh, nephew of Mirza Ali Khan Amin al-Dowleh and brother of Hassan Khan Vossough al-Dowleh, was born in 1873/1252. He was initially an aide to Nasser al-Din Shah. Given the title of Monshi-Hozour (1897/1276), Dabir-Hozour, Vazir-Hozour, and finally Ghavam al-Saltaneh, he held the following posts: vice minister of the interior (1909–10/1288–89), vice minister of war (1910/1289), minister of war (1910/1289), minister of justice (1911/1290), minister of the interior (1911–12/1290–91), minister of finance (1917/1296), minister of the interior (1917–18/1296–97),

became prime minister and founded the Democrat party—and the communists. First of all, he had brought in two or three communist ministers, including Dr. Kechavarz[62] into his cabinet.[63]

I remember one day, they [members of the two parties] had a terrible fight in the streets. Mozaffar Firouz,[64] who was governor-general of Khorasan, Sistan, and Baluchestan (1918–21/1296–1300), arrested by Prime Minister Seyyed Zia Tabatabai (1921/130), prime minister (1921–22/1300 and 1922–23/1301). He was arrested in 1923/1302 for an alleged plot against Prime Minister Reza Khan, and his estates were confiscated. He was released and banished to Europe (October 1923/1302), but allowed to return to Iran (March 1929/1307) when he went to reside on his property in Lahijan until Reza Shah's abdication (1941/1320). During the reign of Mohammad-Reza Shah, Ghavam was prime minister (1942–43/1321, 1946–47/1324–26, and 1952/1331). Although he was considered by some to be pro-British early in his career in the 1940s/1320s), the British found him to be too independent. He was, however, thought to favor increased American influence in Iran, believing that it was the only means of keeping Iran free of foreign domination.

[62] Dr. Fereydoun Kechavarz, son of Mohammad Vakil al-Tojjar Yazdi (merchant and Majles deputy). University education in France, physician, leader of the Tudeh Party, Fourteenth Majles deputy from Bandar Pahlavi, and minister of education (1946/1325). Fled from Iran in 1949/1327, lived in the Soviet Union, Iraq, Algeria, and Switzerland. Published a book entitled, *Man Mottaham Mikonam* (Tehran: Ravagh Press, 1979). See his memoirs in the Harvard Iranian Oral History Collection.

[63] Ahmad Ghavam shuffled his cabinet on 3 August 1946 (12 Mordad 1325), bringing in three members of the Tudeh party: Dr. Fereydoun Kechavarz, Education; Iraj Eskandari, Commerce and Industries; and Dr. Morteza Yazdi, Health.

[64] Mozaffar Firouz, grandson of Abdolhossein Farmanfarma and son of Daftarolmolouk and Firouz Firouz (Nosrat al-Dowleh), was born in Kermanshah in 1905/1284 and sent to England at the age of six. He studied at Harrow and Cambridge. He was editor of the

deputy prime minister and also a cousin of Mossadegh, came [to the hospital] and very, very imperiously said, "Open the door." I said, "Why?" "My children (he meant the members of his party) have been wounded and they have to be hospitalized." I said, "I'm sorry. We cannot have that. This is the result of fighting—street fighting. This is a hospital for surgery, for midwifery and we cannot have you." So he insisted. I said, "Okay, you wait."

He came [in] and we put the mattresses [on the floor]. (We had plenty of mattresses in the cellar.) We brought them up, [and] put these people [on them]. I called Professor Adl to come. [In the meantime] these men [Mozaffar Firouz and his assistants] started, you know, showing off. Across [from] our hospital was the famous Park Hotel which was a very elegant gathering place. [Firouz told us], "Send to the Park Hotel for dinner for the children. Give them dinner!" I said, "Well, you know, in a hospital the kitchen closes, at the latest, at seven o'clock. I have nothing." They said, "Well, you must feed them." I said, "You like them so much, go and buy them some

---

newspaper *R'ad-e Emruz* (1943/1322), and was instrumental in bringing back Seyyed Zia Tabatabai to Iran from exile in Palestine (1943/1322). He served as assistant to Prime Minister Ahmad Ghavam (1946/1325), was first minister of labor and propaganda (1946/1325), and ambassador to the Soviet Union (1946–7/1325–26). He spent the rest of his life in exile in Paris, France, where he died in 1987/1366. See his memoirs in the Harvard Iranian Oral History Collection.

food at the Park Hotel. They deserve it!"

[Firouz] started giving [orders]. I said, "Look here, you! Shut up! I don't care who you are. And this fighting wasn't so wonderful, because all of your so-called children are wounded in the back which shows that they were running away and not facing the fight." He stopped. He wanted also to complain to his cousin, Dr. Mossadegh. It didn't come to anything. That was the atmosphere. I wasn't very much interested in politics. I didn't understand much of it. I was expecting my third child and I had a little [pause].

The Najmiyeh Foundation was founded by Dr. Mossadegh's mother. The foundation in turn owned the Najmiyeh Hospital which was always supposed to treat ten patients free [of charge]. They also had [a number of] houses, the revenue of which went to this foundation. The foundation was originally made to look after ten poor people medically. Also, they had built many rooms [which they] rented as a hospital [room] to any doctor who wanted to take it, provided that he [agreed to] also treat the poor patients for [free]. The foundation paid [the doctors] ten tomans a day for every patient—that was three thousand tomans a month. Okay?

When I came back to the hospital, [I noticed that] we had ten beds for men only. [There] was [a terrace] over the kitchen, and it was the only place where we could have hot water, because there was a big range in the kitchen. So, I asked Mossadegh al-Saltaneh to let me build a few showers on the terrace. [We needed the showers] because [most of] these [patients] were peasants and came full of lice. We [also] had a typhus epidemic in Iran, because of the Poles. The Poles, who had been kept in camps in Russia and were going through Iran to be settled all over the world, brought all kinds of diseases with them. We had many, many cases of typhus and it was spread, you know, through lice and we didn't want to have that. To say nothing of the fact of having a young mother find lice on her bed. And [Dr. Mossadegh] refused [to build the showers].

Then I asked him to allow me to increase the number of beds for the poor, because Tehran was in a terrible situation economically. There were so many people from the provinces and everybody was so poor—life was very expensive. And we had [a] little fight over that. I said, "When your mother founded this hospital, Tehran was a small city. People used to walk [instead of drive]. There [were] no cars. I'm sure if she lived now, she would understand that you have to increase [the number of rooms]." "No. No. No. Nothing doing," he said.

[In the meantime, there were] two chaps that [periodically] came from the foundation. One came every day to write the name of all the free patients. The other [man] was a kind of bailiff. Mossadegh [like] every [other] big landowner had someone who looked after [his] land. This fellow, when he came, would always look all around. He asked questions. He was a kind of spy and I didn't like that at all. In the end,

Mossadegh found that he wasn't so good and they separated.

There were also two nurses—two sisters—whom I didn't like very much. One day I told Mossadegh. "You wanted me back in your hospital because I suppose you trust me." He said, "Of course I trust you." I said, "Why do you [then] spy on me?" He said, "I don't." I said, "Yes, you do. Ask me anything you want [yourself]." He said, "No. No. I'm sorry." I said, "No. Please ask me. You know, the trouble with a spy is that when he doesn't find anything, he invents. And this is where the trouble starts." He said okay. I told the two nurses, "You know, you work here. You don't spy, please. Why spy here? This is a hospital. I'm running it, and it's open. There is no underground activity [here]." That was that.

So, I realized that Mossadegh, like many other important people—[such as] the shah in his own way, and others that I don't want to name, especially if they are a little bit dictatorial or have great authority—are always in the hands of the so-called "entourage." You know the famous saying of one of the Roman emperors, Caesars, who said, "Rome (meaning the whole empire) trembles before the name of Caesar. Caesar trembles before his wife. And both his wife and he tremble before their child." You see? I think [this saying] demonstrates the fact that all big men have this weakness (which we don't realize) of giving part of their will and authority to people who don't deserve it. And these people are the ones who cause all the trouble.

Ghavam al-Saltaneh

HL: How about Ghavam al-Saltaneh? Did you ever meet him?

FP: Yes. I met him [when] he became prime minister. I must say here that I was great friends with Dr. Iran Alam[65] and her sister, Touran Alam, and also with their mother. When I came back to Iran, *Khanom* [Mrs.] Amiralam and Dr. Amiralam[66] were like mother and father to me. Amiralam was the eldest daughter of Vossough al-Dowleh, who was the brother of Ghavam al-Saltaneh. Whereas Vossough al-Dowleh was a courteous, nice and wonderful person and a poet, his brother was very, very stern and very strict. The first thing Ghavam

---

[65] Iran Aalam was born in 1914/1293 in Tehran. She received her medical degree in Paris, was professor at the Faculty of Medicine, Tehran University and head of the Maternity Department, Reza Hospital.

[66] Dr. Amirkeivan Amiralam (Alam al-Dowleh) was the son of Haj Mirza Ali-Akbar Motamed al-Vozara, Iranian consul in Damascus. Amiralam was educated at Damascus, Beirut, and Lyons, where he obtained a medical degree. He began private practice in Tehran (1911/1290), and was an army doctor for some years. He married the eldest daughter of Hassan Vossough al-Dowleh, and took part in politics through the influence of his father-in-law. He reorganized the shrine hospital at Mashhad and was Second Majles deputy from Tehran, minister of commerce and public works (1920/1299), Fourth and Fifth Majles deputy from Mashhad, minister of education, endowments and fine arts (1921–22/1300–1301). He represented Dargaz at the constituent assembly of 1925/1304 and voted in favor of dynasty change. He was Seventh Majles deputy from Dargaz, Eighth and Ninth Majles deputy from Shahrud. He was the personal physician of Reza Shah and minister of health (1948/1327). He helped to found the Red Lion and Sun Association. He was appointed to the First through the Third Senate from Tehran.

al-Saltaneh did when he became prime minister was [to decree that] no Iranian official was allowed to accept invitations from foreign embassies.

The only time I met him was when Ghavam al-Saltaneh was prime minister, and his nephew, Ali Vossough, [was getting] married. There was a big, big wedding reception at the Officer's Club [*bashgah-e afsaran*, باشگاه افسران]. I was a young, a very young, woman at the time.

General Haj-Ali Razmara

HL: How about Razmara?

FP: Razmara. Well, I also met him from far. Razmara was head of the General Staff when we were in Pakistan for the first time.[67] He was the one who sent the cable to my husband saying, "Come back immediately, because you've been appointed chief of G-2." To which my husband replied, "Please explain to His Majesty that I'm much too young in rank and inexperienced. And I'll make so many enemies in this job that I will be paralyzed." [Nevertheless], he accepted [the position]. Razmara liked my husband very much.

I met him from [a distance] while he was prime minister.[68] I remember him as a small man, always very clean-looking.

---

[67] Pakravan's first assignment in Pakistan was in 1949–50 (1328–29).

[68] General Haj-Ali Razmara was prime minister from 26 June 1950 to 7 March 1951 (5 Tir to 16 Esfand 1329) when he was assassinated.

He always seemed to be coming out of his bath. Very energetic-looking. But I didn't know him. I think I never even spoke with him.

HL: And General Zahedi?

FP: No. I never met—or perhaps I met him once, I don't remember. I don't remember at all, unless I met him at some reception, but not to speak to.

Former Queen Soraya

HL: How about former Queen Soraya?

FP: My mother-in-law was lady-in-waiting to Princess Shams,[69] and we used to go to the court very often. And when my husband was chief of G-2 during the time of Mossadegh, the shah used to invite us to private parties which lasted usually twelve hours.

HL: Twelve hours?

FP: Lasted twelve hours, you know. For instance, if we went for dinner at eight o'clock, then we finished by having breakfast at Shahvand in Sadabad[70] at eight o'clock to see the sun rise.

---

[69] Princess Shams Pahlavi was the eldest child of Reza Shah and his second wife, Tajolmolouk. Princess Shams married Fereydoun Djam (later General Djam), son of Prime Minister Mahmoud Djam in 1936/1315 and Ezzatollah Minbashian (later called Mehrdad Pahlbod) in 1946/1325. She was vice chairman of the Red Lion and Sun Association.

[70] Sadabad was the royal compound north of Shemiran where the shah and his family maintained residential palaces. Shahvand was one such palace.

HL: Really?

FP: It was [a] very, very childish party. We used to dance, play musical chairs, have dinner, play guessing games. It was really not at all the orgies of the oriental court. It was very nice.

And I didn't like Soraya, because I found her very, very cold, very distant. I never spoke to her until they [the shah and Soraya] came on a state visit to India, where we were.[71] They stayed three weeks, and so we traveled with them all over the place. They left India through Bombay.

When my husband and I were coming back to Delhi by train, there was a lady who had been appointed as lady-in-waiting to Soraya during her stay in India. (Her husband was the former nawab of Rampour and a member of the Indian parliament.) She was absolutely kicking mad. She said, "[Soraya] has no manners." She said this. [Soraya] upset the protocol all the time. For instance, when you had to wear long and formal dress, she would say, "No. I don't have the patience."

The mayor of Bombay was a woman and she gave a fantastic luncheon reception for ladies, while the shah was visiting some navy unit. I think even the governor was a woman, I don't remember very well. Anyway, we Iranians were very few. Besides the queen, there were her two ladies-in-waiting, and there was me. Perhaps the wife of our ambassador [was there]. I'm not sure.

---

[71] Pakravan was military attaché in India 1954–57 (1333–35).

As a result, I was seated quite close to the queen and this Indian lady. (The Indian women have a very, very strong feeling of their importance when they acquire public office.) [The Indian lady] made a speech, a very long, nice speech. I think there were at least a thousand women there. Many, many women, perhaps five hundred, I don't know. I have no way to judge. [After the speech] everybody waited for the queen, the empress, to get up and reply to this speech. She [just] sat.

I talked to Mrs. [Morteza] Yazdanpanah, I said, "*Khanom*, tell Her Majesty to reply." Then [I said], "Your Majesty, will you reply?" She said, "No." I said, "Please. I beg you, Your Majesty. Do get up and reply." She said, "What shall I say?" I said, "Say thank you. Say a few words. [Say] you've been impressed." [She said], "No." She got up and went.

And so, during all that trip from Bombay to Delhi until night, that woman, the lady-in-waiting, said, "Yes, she has no manners. Why did she refuse to wear formal clothes? If she'd been invited to the Buckingham Palace, do you think she would do as she wished?" I said, "Well, you know, the climate, and [all that]." And the woman said, "No. No. No." I said, "Well [pause]." I had to defend my queen. Anyway.

But, I pitied [Soraya] very much, because I think she was the woman that the king loved the most and she couldn't give him a child.

HL: Is it true that he really loved her?

FP: Oh yes! He was very much [in love with her]. My

mother-in-law told me a little anecdote. She said [once] they were having a small lunch—a few people. Soraya smoked. (And I saw myself at one of these evenings that she smoked.) And the king was like a young lover. He would look through all his pockets and immediately give her the lighter. He adored her. And my mother-in-law said [Soraya] was mad. I said, "What happened?" She said, "You know, we started to speak about [the ideal woman] for a man. We asked the shah what was his ideal beauty in woman. And he said, 'Well, I'm very lucky, because the queen is exactly the kind of woman that I like.' And [Soraya] said, 'Well, I cannot say the same for Your Majesty.'" Now whether Soraya was joking or she was serious, I don't know, [but] my mother-in-law was very, very mad.

And then Soraya went and wrote this stupid book.[72] So silly, you know. Practically saying that they were so poor that she had to vacuum [pause]. No. She didn't say that, but I mean it was very, very low.

HL: Yet, as you know there are people who say that Soraya was a good queen and claim that it was after his divorce that the shah began to go astray.

FP: They have to prove that. I don't know. The thing is that when Soraya was the queen, she was very popular, because Iranians are very sensitive to beauty. She was beautiful. She's

---

[72] Soraya Esfandiary, *The Autobiography of H.I.H. Princess Soraya* (London: Arthur Barker Limited, 1963).

not my kind of beauty. I don't like cold people. She was very shy, actually. I remember when she was in Bombay, we went to another lunch for ladies at Poona. She was extremely shy. I don't think she was proud and arrogant. She was shy. Another thing I know is that she hated to be a queen.

HL: She hated to be queen?

FP: Several times she tried—that's what my mother-in-law said— to persuade the king to abdicate and go live abroad.

HL: Really?

FP: Yes. She didn't like it at all. I must say that the life of the court and all the intrigues between [pause]. The shah had too many brothers and too many sisters. That's not good for a king. That's not good at all.

So I think [Soraya] is to be pitied, because she didn't succeed in giving [the shah] a child. She didn't succeed. Another thing that I know for a fact is that she wasn't very kind to the shah's daughter, Shahnaz.[73] For those who knew, it wasn't very pleasant. The shah liked his daughter so much. I was witness to that. Then he stopped. He completely cut her off, because Soraya didn't like her. This wasn't very nice.

---

[73] Princess Shahnaz Pahlavi, the shah's first child from the marriage with former Queen Fawzieh of Egypt. She was educated in Switzerland and married Ardeshir Zahedi on 8 September 1957 (17 Shahrivar 1336) which led to the birth of Princess Mahnaz. The marriage, however, ended in divorce several years later. She married Khosrow Jahanbani in the 1970s/1350s.

Atmosphere at the Court

HL: What was it like at the court? There are all kinds of rumors and stories, but nobody has really described it.

FP: I'll tell you something. I was recently at a lunch with people who were very close to the court, and they started saying things which surprised me very much. Then they [asked me], "Where were you? Why don't you know these things?" I told them, "First of all, I was working practically all my life. I worked. Then I had my children."

My children went before my work, but still, I mean, I devoted my time to my work, to my job, to my close friends. I wasn't the type. I liked social life. I liked to put [on] beautiful dresses and to go to a ball, and to go to an embassy or to a big important reception, but it wasn't my life. And my husband never discussed his job with me except on things that were common knowledge, public knowledge. That was for my safety, and also because we had many other subjects of conversation.

So, I told these women, "Look here. I was always working. I never was in the confidence of people who gossiped, because I never liked gossip." Well, as an English friend of mine used to say, "Small bits of juicy gossip, yes, but real gossip, judging people and accusing them without any proof, no."

I remember one day when I was still very naive, a friend of mine, an acquaintance, said, "Well, how do you know So-and-so [doesn't] sleep with so-and-so? Don't you live in this town?" I said, "Were you there when they did it?" I said, "You know, depending on who is watching, you can find yourself in circumstances that are judged to be very bad or to be very innocent."

And besides I hated this spreading of rumors and all that. I remember a few months before this revolution started, I begged [my friends]. [By repeating rumors], I said, "You're serving Khomeini, because you are like a *tabl* [طبل], a drum. He beats on you and you produce a sound."

So I wouldn't know, at all, all the rumors. I knew what my mother-in-law told me. She used to go [to the court] very often. I used to go to Princess Shams's every two weeks. She had a reception with a lecture or music, and things like that. The only time we were—I shouldn't say—intimate [was when] we were going to the shah's court during the short period [when] my husband was chief of G-2 during Mossadegh's time.

HL: How about the period when General Pakravan was head of the Security Organization?

FP: Well, we used to go, but from 1958 [1337 onward] our court became very, very formal.

HL: Please explain.

Queen Farah, the Early Years

FP: The court became very, very formal. I'll give you a small example. The first visit abroad of Queen Farah with her husband was to inaugurate an art exhibition in Paris— "Persian Art,

7,000 Years of Art." My eldest daughter, [Saideh], was a student at the time in Paris. And Parviz Adl, the counselor for press affairs, was responsible [for the visit]. Because he liked my husband very much, he asked my daughter to be one of the hostesses at this museum where the exhibition was [held]. And the queen came and saw Saideh. [The queen] is a bit older. They always followed each other in the same school with two years of difference. [The queen] came back and said, "Saideh, is that you?" She was extremely nice. She said to Jahanbani,[74] "I want Saideh Pakravan to be invited to all the receptions that she can attend, except the Elysée[75] and things like that."

And when [the queen] came back [to Iran], it was the custom, the protocol, that all the officials go to the airport to greet Their Majesties. She was shaking hands with somebody. After she shook hands with me, she turned and said, "You know, I saw Saideh very often in Paris." I said, "Yes, I know. Your Majesty has been extremely kind."

And, [while the queen was] a young girl and a student, whenever my husband came to Paris, he used to take her out for dinner with Madame Helleu, who was a friend of hers and the head of the Franco-Iranian Association. So, whenever she saw my husband, she used to wink at him and say, "Remember, I was a student and now [I am the queen]."

I remember long before she became queen, [my husband]

---

[74] Massoud Jahanbani, Iran's ambassador to France.

[75] Elysée Palace, residence of the French president.

said, "Oh, by the way, I had dinner with Madame Helleu and Farah." I said, "Oh, how is she?" He said, "She didn't speak very much. I suppose as a young girl, she was very impressed by a general with white hair. But I think she has a very, very, very strong personality." That was before she became queen.

But after that, she wasn't allowed to speak to anybody. They were very impressed when the queen of England came to Iran on an official visit,[76] [and] after the dinner she and Prince Philip just mingled with the people. Then, I heard from the British ambassador, who said, "Every member of the royal family makes a point of seeing as many people and talking to as many people as possible—to give that feeling of, 'Ah, I spoke to Princess Margaret or to the queen or to Prince Philip.'" And the shah was very, very much impressed by that, so after that he used to do that [mingle]. But always he kept a distance between himself and the Iranians.

HL: Was this after 1958 [1337]?

FP: Oh, this was in the 1960s [1340s after] Queen [Elizabeth came].

HL: You said the court became more formal after 1958 [1337].

FP: Yes, '58, '59 [1337–38]. It becomes very, very formal. Later on, I heard that Hossein Loghman-Adham[77] had been

---

[76] On 2 March 1961 (11 Esfand 1339) Queen Elizabeth of England and Prince Philip arrived in Tehran on an official visit.

[77] Dr. Hossein Loghman-Adham, son of Loghman al-Dowleh (physician), received his university education in medicine and was

sent to the court of England to learn real royal protocol. And they really had too much of it. The court became very stiff, very formal, and it wasn't [pause]. I don't like protocol. I like protocol a little bit, because it's easier when you know exactly where you stand in official circumstances, but not so that it's stifling. No. What's the point? After all, we're all human beings, and I think we can respect a person without being completely paralyzed by all kinds of rules. Well, that was that. What else?

Princess Ashraf

HL: Is there anything you'd like to say about Princess Ashraf?[78]

FP: My sister had better relations with Princess Ashraf and knew her better. When Princess Shams was the vice president of the Iranian Red Cross (the president was the shah himself), she married Mr. Pahlbod against the will of her brother. So, she was deprived officially of all her titles and of course all the privileges she had; and the vice presidency of the Red Cross was given to Princess Ashraf.

I was a member of [the Red Cross] and used to go there until the shah forgave his sister, and [Princess Shams] came back to Iran. [The shah] wanted to give back her job as vice president of the Red Cross.

Ninth through Thirteenth Majles deputy from Tehran.

[78] Princess Ashraf Pahlavi, twin sister of Mohammad-Reza Shah, was born in Tehran in 1919/1298. She married Ali Ghavam, son of Ghavam al-Molk (1937/1316), Ahmad Chafik (Shafiq) (1944/1323), and later Mehdi Boushehri. She was chairman of the Imperial Social Services Organization and the Women's Organization.

So in the end I left. I don't remember if I told Princess Ashraf or if I had somebody tell her that "I cannot be in this false position. My mother-in-law is lady-in-waiting [with Princess Shams]. I am with you. [If] anything happens between the two [of you], you will feel that it's either I or my mother-in-law who has been making some trouble."

Princess Ashraf was extremely nice. I must say that mostly I found out how nice she was when I became responsible in part for tourism in Iran. She wanted me very much to cooperate with her husband, Dr. Boushehri,[79] who also had a kind of private tourist organization and an agency. She was extremely nice.

Then when we came to Paris [to head the embassy], she was very, very nice. She tried to smooth our way. She knew that we were not familiar with all the intrigues of the court. So several times she told me to do this and that, to be careful. She was extremely nice. Now, here she is [living in exile].

I pity her terribly, because I think the book she wrote, *Faces in the Mirror*,[80] is a beautiful book. It's not always truthful, unfortunately, because I suppose nobody is ever [fully] truthful. But, I think what happened to her, you know, as a twin very attached to her brother. She lost her son, Shahryar,[81]

---

[79] Mehdi Boushehri, husband of Princess Ashraf.

[80] Ashraf Pahlavi, *Faces in a Mirror: Memoirs from Exile* (Englewood Cliffs, NJ: 1980).

[81] Shahryar Chafik, son of Princess Ashraf, was a naval officer assassinated in Paris on 7 December 1979 (16 Azar 1358). Sheikh

who was a wonderful person, a wonderful person. She lost her brother and she lost her mother. They say her mother was mummified. Never mind. It was her mother. And she helps, I hear. I haven't seen her since the revolution, but I hear that she helps Iranians [financially] very, very much.

I think one thing that cannot be denied is her courage. They accuse her of having taken money, but a friend of mine told me something very interesting. She said when Mossadegh was prime minister, he asked the shah to send his sister away, and she was practically kicked out of the country with nothing. The son that was [recently] assassinated, [Shahryar], was a small baby and was in treatment in Switzerland. They suspected that he had TB—tuberculosis. And Mossadegh cut—that's the story—cut the money to send to him until he had the proof that [his illness] was genuine.

And anyway, that friend of mine, who was very close to Princess Ashraf, said that one day she went to see her in a very small hotel where she stayed in Paris. And she had put a few knickknacks, jewelry, very cheap jewelry, on the bed. And she told my friend, "You know, I was kicked [out] like a servant from [my] house. I wasn't even allowed to take any of my things. This is all I was able to bring with me. And my friend in Paris helps me to live, because I have no money at all. But, I swear in front of you, that if ever the situation turns back, I shall become a very, very, very rich person."

One thing that people always forget is that none of the
_____
Sadegh Khalkhali and Fadaiyan-e Islam took responsibility for the

royal family has received a proper, formal higher education. You [must] remember that Ashraf is a self-made woman (she tells this in her book). Her father didn't want her to go to university. She's really intelligent. She learned French beautifully. She learned English beautifully. She learned many, many things. She was too eager, because she wanted to serve her brother. Anyway, it's very sad. I have no judgment there, because I think I shouldn't judge a person who has suffered as much as she has.

Queen Farah, the Later Years

HL: How about the former queen, Queen Farah?
FP: Queen Farah—I knew her as a young child. I knew her father and mother very well. She was an only child. I think it's funny that her father used to call her "crown of my head" *taj-e saram* [تاج سرم] and her mother's real name is Taj al-Molouk, it means the "crown of the kings." I don't know, I really cannot say, because my impression was that she was very popular in Iran. I never saw her informally since she became queen, except once. No. I'm forgetting that she came to Pakistan. They came several times.

The first time she came—after those who came to greet her—she [and the shah] settled in the house that was put at their disposal. She called me in and we walked a little bit. She was very fond of trees and asked me about trees in Pakistan which are beautiful. She asked me about several things. But I action.

was never close to her, so I really cannot say.

I see her mother when she's in Paris. I saw Queen Farah last June.[82] It was the first time we had seen each other after the revolution and we cried. She kissed me. I kissed her. We cried. Then she said that she wants to live a very, very retired life with her children. She doesn't want to mix in any public things. She expressed a wish to live in France, because the French are always very kind to her. You know, I told her, "You are a bit their queen. They always call you 'Farah Diba.'"

"Yes," she laughed. She likes France.

But people say that she organized all these big festivals, all these big events that, in the end, drove people mad: the coronation,[83] the Persepolis.[84] I remember when there was talk of celebrating the Twenty-five Centuries of Continuous Monarchy in Iran, I was a member of the small committee called the reception committee and *tashrifat* [تشریفات, protocol]. We used to have meetings every week and we never achieved anything. We always changed our plans. In the end, I think we all agreed to celebrate this big, important event in our history by having an enormous congress of orientalists in Iran—which

---

[82] June 1982 (Khordad–Tir 1361).

[83] On 26 October 1967 (4 Aban 1346) Mohammad-Reza Shah crowned himself and Empress Farah in the Golestan Palace.

[84] On 12 October 1971 (20 Mehr 1350) celebrations marking 2,500 years of Persian monarchy were held in Persepolis, near Shiraz. In response to critical reports regarding the cost of the event, a government spokesman said the celebration had cost $16.6 million, charging that some publications had totally exaggerated the figures.

[would] have been much better than to have what we had. Then I went to Pakistan, so they changed it.

I remember Mr. Boushehri—that means Amirhomayoun,[85] an old man, who presided over our meetings. One day we told him, "Tell His Majesty that we think this and that." He said, "Me? Tell His Majesty that the committee has this kind or this opinion?" We said, "Yes. Of course. Why not?" He said, "Never." I said, "Look here, Mr. Boushehri. If His Majesty wanted to settle everything himself, why should he have committees? If he wants committees, it's because we were supposed to give advice." "No. No. No. Nothing doing."

I really wouldn't know what kind of a person she [Queen Farah] is. I am sure that she was impatient. I remember one day we saw her before we left for Pakistan, and she said, "I'm

---

[85] Javad Boushehri-Dehdashti (Amirhomayoun), was the second son of Haj Agha Mohammad Moin al-Tojjar (merchant and Majles deputy). Amirhomayoun was educated in Tehran and Europe and married a daughter of Haj Amin al-Zarb. He represented Tehran at the constituent assembly of 1925/1304 and voted in favor of dynasty change. He was elected to the Seventh and Eighth Majles from Tehran (1928–33/1307–12). A British Foreign Office report described him as "More interested in politics than his elder brother Agha Reza, fond of pomp, and very extravagant in his manner of living. Nicknamed by some of his friends 'Prince Merchant.'" (See "Report on Personalities in Persia, 1940," British Foreign Office, 371/24582 (E 832/826/34). Hereafter: "Report on Personalities.") He spent some time in Europe, returning in 1943/1322. Subsequently he was a member of the Election Supervisory Board (1943/1322), arrested by the occupying forces (1943/1322), minister of post and telegraph (1947/1326), minister of agriculture (1948/1327), and minister of roads (1951–52/1330–31). He was elected to the First (resigned on 1 December 1951/9 Azar 1330), Fourth, and Fifth Senate from Tehran, and appointed to the Second and Third Senate from Shiraz, and Sixth Senate from Tehran.

so eager to help His Majesty. I'm so eager to make Iran, our history, our civilization, our arts known all over the world. But, I have often the impression that people don't follow me. I don't know why." So she felt that.

You know, there was a lack of understanding of what people really wanted. Although I'm not left-minded or anything, but practical, I think that she should never have allowed them to set apart a school for her children. The crown prince should have gone to a public school. He should have been kicked and he should have kicked.

I remember one day, I criticized [the school arrangement] in front of some [people] who were close to her. They said, "Oh well, but you know in this school they have the son of the gardener and the son of the cook and the son of the [pause]." I said, "Look here. They still are the gardener of the court and the cook of the court. He must meet real people. He should go to a public school. He should have friends who are not from the court." I think that was a mistake.

I really don't know what to say about her, because she was very popular. What strikes me now is that when they say, "Well, Khomeini started to make trouble in the middle of the 1970s [1350s]," [they are wrong]. All the propaganda against the royal family started much, much, much earlier than that. When the queen had her baby at this hospital in the south of the city,[86] I was worried. I said, "My God. They will say that

---

[86] Crown Prince Reza Pahlavi was born on 31 October 1960

it's not her child." Luckily the child looked so much like his father that they stopped saying that.

But I remember the love for the royal family. I remember I was shopping and I saw a young agricultural worker, you know, one of these peasants, walking, coming across the other way and just crying, crying: "*Khanom, khanom*" [Lady, lady]. I thought he was a beggar, or something had happened. I said, "What's the matter with you?" And I saw all the cars [flashing] their lights and hooting and honking [their horns]. I was concentrating on what I was doing. I said, "What's the matter?" He said, "*Khanom*, it's a son. It's a son!" I said, "Oh, good for you." I thought he had a son. He said, "No, *Khanom*. Our shah has an heir." The people were so happy when they heard "an heir."

Then, very, very insidiously, they started small rumors here and there. There were, you know, some people who were spreading these rumors. I remember they said that the young prince was deaf-mute. My husband at the time was directing security and used to have an audience with the shah two times a week. After he had met the shah at the Sadabad Palace—where it was more relaxed in the summer—he said, "This time the little boy was on his father's knee, and he spoke French, and he said this and that." [Even though] I knew he wasn't mute, I asked my husband, "So he's not a mute?" He said, "What is that?" I said, "Don't you know? You [are the] head of security!

(9 Aban 1339).

They have spread the rumor that the prince cannot speak, that his hands [are] like those of a duck, and that the queen's ears [are] so large that they had to cut them." They said absolutely anything, anything—the most fantastic rumors.

And they would spread them, and of course it [would spread] from the higher rank of the society down to the smallest village; and it was embellished and enlarged and all that. There were many, many rumors, you know. It was fantastic. We are always ready to believe everything. I always say, "Don't forget that we are the country of *A Thousand and One Nights* tales." We like tales, especially when they concern kings, queens, and princesses.

Hossein Ala

HL: Did you ever meet Mr. Hossein Ala?[87]

---

[87] Hossein Ala was the son of Prince Mohammad-Ali Khan Ala al-Saltaneh. Born in 1884/1263, Ala was educated at Westminster School in England. He was appointed CMG (Companion of the Order of St. Michael and St. George) in 1905/1284 when he accompanied his father on a special mission to London for the coronation of King Edward VII. He was appointed *chef de cabinet* in the Ministry of Foreign Affairs (1906/1285), his father being then minister of foreign affairs. He remained as *chef de cabinet* to various ministers until 1915/1294. Subsequently, he served as minister of public works (1918/1297), accompanied the abortive Iranian mission to the Paris Peace Conference (1918/1297), was minister in Madrid (1919/1298), and in Washington (1920–25/1299–1304). He was elected to the Fifth Majles as deputy from Tehran (he voted against the change of dynasties). During the reign of Reza Shah, he was appointed minister of public works (1927/1306), second delegate to the League of Nations (1928/1307), minister in Paris (1929–33/1308–12), and one of the delegates to represent Iran before the League of Nations in the Anglo-

FP: Yes, many times. You know, Hossein Ala was always in reserve. Whenever the government was upset, and until they found a new prime minister he would fill the interim. He was very nice. He was, you know, known for his puns. In the last years of her life, I knew his wife very well—and his mother. He was very courteous, very learned, and very nice.

HL: Do you know the circumstances under which he left the Ministry of Court?[88]

Persian Oil Company dispute (1933/1312). He returned to Tehran to take over a high post in Bank Melli Iran (1933–34/1312–13), was minister in London (1934–36/1313–15), supervisor of Monopoly Companies (1936/1315), director general of commerce (1937/1316), minister of commerce (1937–39/1316–18), governor of the Bank Melli (1941–42/1320–21), minister of court (1942–45/1321–24), ambassador to the United States and the United Nations (1945–50/1324–29), minister of foreign affairs (1950/1329), prime minister (1951/1329–30), minister of court (1951–53/1330–32), and prime minister (1955–57/1334–36). An attempt was made on his life by Mozaffar-Ali Zolghadar, member of the Fadaiyan-e Islam (1955/1334). He was minister of court (1957–63/1336–42), and appointed senator from Shiraz (1963–64/1342–43). He died on 12 July 1964 (21 Tir 1343). A report written in 1940/1319 by the British Legation in Tehran described him as: "A hard worker and a staunch patriot, intelligent and well-read, interested in the literature of many countries and quite a good pianist. Has a perfect command of English and speaks good French. In the past he has had a reputation for anti-British sentiments; he seems a good deal more anti-Russian than anti-British, and is doubtless more pro-Persian than either." See "Report on Personalities."

[88] According to Marvin Zonis, by the second day of the rioting following the arrest of Ayatollah Khomeini in June 1963 (Khordad 1342), many participants had been killed by the security forces. Hossein Ala, then minister of court, expressed concern over the force of the military reaction to the riots. He called together Abdollah Entezam, chairman of the National Iranian Oil Company; General Morteza Yazdanpanah, chief of the Imperial Inspectorate; and Reza Hekmat (Sardar Fakher), president of the Majles. "Together they agreed that

FP: No. No. I don't remember. When was that?

HL: It was in June 1963 [Khordad 1342]. It is said that after the 15th of Khordad [5 June 1963] riots,[89] he and some others met and discussed [interruption]?

FP: I don't. I don't know, really. I wouldn't know. I really don't remember. One thing I can tell you, [even if] I [meant] to speak to him or to discuss [a subject] with him, he would never [respond]. He was the type who wouldn't discuss [such subjects] with a woman of my age. He was of the old school. But I can tell you that I don't believe he was the type to intrigue against the shah. I don't know. It was in 1962, 1963 [1341, 1342]?

HL: Yes, 1963 [1342].

FP: I don't know. I really don't know.

Dr. Manouchehr Eghbal

HL: And Dr. Eghbal?[90] Did you know him?

the savage military response to what had begun as a simple protest against the arrest of Khomeini could only redound to the ill of His Majesty." They decided to approach the shah to urge him to temper the government's response. "These four devoted elite officials carried their forebodings to His Imperial Majesty at a hastily arranged audience." The shah reacted angrily to this initiative. Ala was relieved of his duties as minister of court and moved to the Senate. Yazdanpanah was dropped from the Imperial Inspectorate and given a seat in the Senate. Hekmat was forbidden to campaign for the Majles and remained inactive for the rest of his career. Entezam was retired from the National Iranian Oil Company and sent home. See Marvin Zonis, *The Political Elite of Iran* (Princeton: Princeton University Press, 1971), pp. 62–6.

[89] On 15 Khordad 1342 (5 June 1963).

Memoirs of Fatemeh Pakravan

FP: I knew him very, very well. He used to call me *khanom-e khanom-ha* [خانم خانم ها, lady of the ladies]. Dr. Eghbal, you know, was a physician—specialist in the parasitic diseases. He used to bring his patients to Najmiyeh Hospital. I used to pull his leg, because he became minister of post and telegraph, and then minister of things that had nothing to do with his specialty. And as a prime minister—I know he remained a long time—if he achieved anything special, I cannot say. At least he kept the country safe and sound. Whenever he was prime minister—I think he became prime minister twice, I'm not sure—people felt safe. And I mean every class of people, not only the top class. Things were running smoothly without any big declarations, big movements. I knew him very well. I'm glad he died before all the troubles started, because he was so devoted to his country and to public service. He was [also] ambitious. That's [for] sure.

---

[90] Dr. Manouchehr Eghbal was the son of Aboutorab Eghbal al-Tawlieh (Moghbel al-Saltaneh). Born in 1909/1288, Dr. Eghbal was trained as a physician in Paris, France. His posts included: vice minister of health (1943–44/1322–23), acting minister of health (1944/1323), minister of health (1946/1325), minister of post and telegraph (1946/1325), minister of health (1946–47/1325–26), minister of education (1948/1327), minister of roads (1948/1327), minister of health (1948–49/1327–28), minister of the interior (1949/1328), minister of roads (1950/1329), minister of court (1956–57/1335–36), and prime minister (1957–60/1336–39). He was also elected to the Twentieth Majles from Mashhad (1961/1340), and the Second Senate from Tehran. His last major post was chairman of the board and managing director, National Iranian Oil Company (1963–77/1342–56). He died on 25 November 1977 (4 Azar 1356) at the age of 68 of a heart attack.

I remember he had a terrible fight with [Hassan-Ali] Mansour.[91] They nearly came to [a] fist fight at a reception at the Officer's Club. A few days later, there was a dinner party at the French Embassy, and I was seated beside him. He described [their] big [fight]. He said, "You know, it's fantastic! I trained Mansour. I made him what he is. How dare he speak to me like that in public?"

Then after dinner, he took me aside, to a small sofa, and the whole evening he talked to me. I was so embarrassed, because I [thought], "My goodness, they will think that I'm speaking about my husband's job or something like that [with him]." Everybody was careful not to come near [us]. He said, "You know, I cannot stand to be humiliated like that. After all, I have held every high office in this country." (The next day, he sent by messenger a booklet in three languages—French, English, and Persian—listing all his decorations, all his career, and all that.) After the reception in the car, my husband and I [conducted] what we called a "postmortem." I told him [what]

---

[91] Hassan-Ali Mansour was the son of Ali Mansour (Mansour al-Saltaneh), former prime minister. Mansour completed his university education in political science and economics. His posts included: chief of staff of Prime Minister Ala, secretary of the High Economic Council, managing director of the Iran Insurance Company, minister of labor (1959–60/1338–39), minister of commerce (1960/1339), founder of the Progressive Association [Kanun-e Moteraqi, کانون مـتـرقی], the nucleus from which the Iran Novin Party was formed (1962/1341), Twenty-first Majles deputy from Tehran, prime minister (1964–65/1342–43). He was subject to an assassination attempt in front of the Majles building, on 21 January 1965 (1 Bahman 1343). He died a few days later.

Dr. Eghbal [had] told me. He said, "No. No. No. He has not held every high office in this country. He never became chief of staff!"

Dispute over Doubling the Price of Fuel

This fight with Mansour was over the sudden increase in the price of kerosene and gasoline in the middle of the winter. My husband was [also] mad. He went to the shah and said, "How can you allow them to suddenly double [the price of fuel], when three-quarters of the people of this country cook their food, [fuel their vehicles, and] heat [their homes] with kerosene, gasoline, and oil?

Eghbal told me [that during] a reception for the ECAFE[92] conference in Tehran, he told Prime Minister Mansour, "I think you've been a bit harsh. Don't you think that you should have at least telephoned me, as head of the National Oil Company, to see if it was a good time for such an increase?"

HL: You mean the price of fuel was increased without the knowledge of the head of the oil company, and the head of the Security Organization?

FP: No. No. No. No. No. No. Because my husband said—I remember [when] the shah saw Hassan, he asked him,"What have you done to the prime minister? He came here almost crying." And Hassan [had] said, "Well, I had a big fight with

---

[92] ECAFE is the acronym for the United Nations Economic Committee for Asia and the Far East.

him." (Mansour used to tell me, "*Khanom*, I love your husband. If I had been a woman, I would have snatched him [away] from you." Well, compliments.)

My husband went to [Mansour] and made a big scene. He [told him], "I'm in charge of the security of this country. Do you know how much security depends on the well-being of the people? And here you go, in the middle of a very harsh and bad winter increasing, doubling the price of domestic oil and gasoline. Do you want a revolution?"

And you know. People were so mad. There was a saying that taxi-drivers used to say: "I would like to drink Mansour's blood with a small spoon to [prolong] my pleasure." And he was assassinated by these Fadaiyan-e Islam. Nobody seems to attach any importance to the part of the Muslim Brotherhood [*Akhwan al-Muslemin*, اخوان المسلمين].

HL: I find it hard to believe that such a decision could have been made without consultation with these important officials. Was this typical of what you saw in Iran?

Rise of the Technocrats

FP: No. No. It wasn't. It was typical of Mansour, but not of Iran. Mansour was extremely eager to become prime minister—very, very eager. They called all these technocrats *kot-e dow chak* [كت دو چاك], men wearing jackets with two vents]. They very cleverly spread the idea that the time of old-fashioned politicians—of the sage and the wise man—was over. The country must be run by technocrats along technical and economical lines. He was an economic expert, you know.

So he and his friends started. I wouldn't say that he did it or that he wrote a plan, in black and white. But that was the feeling before he became prime minister—that all the people like Eghbal, like Ala, like whoever, were remains from the past, and that they were too much subservient to the shah's will. Not that they were revolutionaries.

You know, it's a fascinating thing to observe that everywhere in the country, the less leftist people are proud to have leftist ideas. It gives them the feeling that they are very open-minded which is a mistake. They're not open-minded. They're just victims of good propaganda.

Anyway, [Mansour's group] spread this word: "Make room for the young people, the young generation. Your time is over." Okay? It had come to the point that really, I would say, all this public opinion was shouting for Mansour to become prime minister. I would say it had come to the point that the shah had no [other] option. The shah was apparently with them. At the time, the shah was wiser. He knew that reversing the whole thing too fast was dangerous.

Doubling the Price of Domestic Oil Products
And so, my husband agreed, everybody agreed that the internal price of the oil products was much, much too low. It wasn't

fair. They, [however], didn't dare to increase it, because not Mossadegh himself, but his entourage had spread the word that if we nationalized oil, every Iranian would receive a can of oil for free and so much money for free. So [the price of] all these products was ridiculously low in Iran. But still, you really have to choose your time. If they had done it in the middle of the summer, people wouldn't have felt it so much. But it was right in the middle of winter in Tehran.

Anyway, he [Mansour] had to go back, so he issued decrees on this. But that was a very, very bad impression and he put himself in terrible danger. Not so much for this oil question, but because he was too modern. And Fadaiyan-e Islam, who had throughout the reign of our late shah assassinated so many people, decided [that] they would assassinate him too.

Assassinations of the 1970s (1350s)

HL: Around 1970, 1971 [1349, 1350], you were in [pause]?

FP: Paris.

HL: You were in Paris. If I remember correctly, that was the time when a number of people were assassinated in Iran. Later on we learned that these assassinations were the work of the Mojahedin[93] and the Cherik-ha-ye Fadaii-e Khalq.[94] Now

---

[93] [سازمان مجاهدین خلق ایران] Sazman-e Mojahedin-e Khalq-e Iran, a Socialist-Islamic organization that opposed the monarchy.

[94] [سازمان چریکهای فدائی خلق ایران], Sazman-e Cherik-ha-ye Fadaii-ye Khalq-e Iran, a Marxist-Leninist organization that opposed the monarchy.

given that your husband had been head of the Security Organization for a number of years, did he have any lingering interest in these events? Was he troubled by these events in Iran? Did he have any thoughts on these events?

FP: Of course he had. Of course he had. First of all because he was a great patriot. And to my shame, I found this out quite late in life. I thought he was like anybody, like all of us—I mean, loving our country. But his love of his country went beyond that. It went with a very high ideal of public service, and a very high ideal of the honor, as he said, of being an officer, a soldier. I really hadn't thought that he was [pause].

He was a military man. He was a soldier in the beautiful sense of the word. He was very, very worried. He knew exactly. He was a great specialist in all these subversion questions. He had studied the thing from close up. And also because as representative of the shah and the [Iranian] government [in France], he was constantly asked, you know, and challenged. Although in France they loved him, they respected him very, very much, still, he was challenged, not as General Hassan Pakravan personally, but as the official representative of his country in France.

And he used to say, "If you use violence, you will meet violence." If these young people don't want to obtain whatever they want [pause]. First of all, we never knew what they wanted. They never said what they wanted. [However], we know [that] in other countries where people have said that they will kill, put bombs, and [conduct] terroristic acts [in order] to obtain democracy, it's not true. We know that for a fact. It's not true at all. [Their real purpose] is to establish another—a very, very bad dictatorship.

So, we were all worried, because it's not very nice to see [stories about these events in newspapers]. They don't do it now. I told several of my newspaper friends, "Whenever there was someone arrested, after they had thrown [bombs, it would immediately appear in your newspapers].

First of all, they [the young people] always threw bombs in public places, killing innocent people. They never tried to kill an important person, never. Those who killed important persons were not the Mojahedin, they were the Fadaiyan-e Islam. They were the fanatical Muslims. So [what the Mojahedin were doing] was something which really didn't appeal to me. I said, "If they really want to kill, why do they kill children? Why do they kill poor women? Why do they kill people who go about their business?"

HL: It sounds like General Pakravan agreed with the way the government was responding to these events.

FP: No. He wasn't. No. No. It wasn't that at all. I don't know what kind of response the government gave: it was to arrest them, it was to put them to death. Most of the time they were killed in fighting, you know, in street fighting. But he [General Pakravan] never agreed with violence for violence's sake. He never agreed with the madness which led people to kill in order to solve problems. He thought it never solved anything. He thought that one has to go to the root [of the problem]. Naturally, these people didn't realize that they were [being] manipulated.

You know, at the same time it's a very simple and a very complex question, this question of terrorism. Don't forget that it was the time when Mao Tse-Tung was extremely popular among all the youth [around] the world. Don't forget that from 1966 [1345] until 1973 [1352]—starting with America—the whole world was experiencing this trouble with their young people and the university people. It was the same in Pakistan.

I remember at the time I asked my husband, "Isn't this funny, Hassan, that this same kind of trouble is arising in countries as different as America, Pakistan, Iran, Jordan, Lebanon, India, and the Philippines? It's as if somebody orchestrated the whole thing." He said, "Yes. It looks like it, doesn't it?" And when I said it to my French friends, they said, "Oh, come on. Come on. You are dreaming. Who is orchestrating that?"

Arnaud de Borchgrave, the head of *Newsweek* in France, was the first to [expose] this disinformation that the Russians had invented and orchestrated. You know they have proof now that all the peace movements, for instance, were (without their own knowledge) financed by the East.

General Nematollah Nassiri

HL: Did General Pakravan ever discuss General Nassiri, his successor at the Security Organization? What did he think of the way he was running it?

FP: First of all, he had no—he didn't really dislike—it was a surprise that he was appointed, because when Alavi-Kia was sent to Germany, the shah said that he wanted Fardoust[95] to become second-in-command, with the title of *qa'em maqam* [قائم مقام, deputy]. And my husband thought it was to prepare Fardoust to eventually replace him, because the head of SAVAK never stayed more than four years in his job. So, he was a bit surprised when Nassiri was nominated.

My husband liked Nassiri as a colleague, [but] he had no reputation for intelligence or any kind of intellectual achievement. He wasn't a man to read. He wasn't a man to [pause]. And he was blindly devoted to the shah. And he was of the same construction as the Mojahedin. You know? That means people who think brutal methods are better than other ways. It's the kind of attitude Iranian fathers have with their children [when they say] "*khafeh Show* [خفه شو], shut up. You're not big enough to say anything." You know, "You're going to get only bread and water."

A Persian child, when he's small, has no right to do anything.

---

[95] General Hossein Fardoust, childhood friend and classmate of Mohammad-Reza Shah, chief of *daftar-e vijeh* [دفتر ویژه, security bureau], deputy chief of SAVAK and head of the Imperial Inspectorate.

Memoirs of Fatemeh Pakravan

He must obey. Well, it was a kind of transfer, you know. He said, "I am in authority. You are young people. You don't understand anything. Shut up or else." So, we didn't have such a great respect for [General Nassiri]. I don't think my husband approved, but he would never criticize [him] publicly. [My husband] had either to [be silent or] criticize [him] publicly and resign. Some people reproached him. They said, "Why didn't you resign?" He said, "If all those who could have an influence on the shah and his policies resigned, we'd leave the whole country to those who influence him in the [wrong] direction."

Nassiri—I don't know. Personally, I didn't like him very much. You see, there is one thing—Nassiri didn't have a good reputation. There was a very sad story of a child of his being [pause]. There were all kinds of stories running. I don't want to repeat them, because I don't believe in spreading rumors, but there is one thing, you know. There is a saying, that the wife of Caesar must be above suspicion. This means that when you are in a responsible position, like the king, the Iranian king, the shah, it does not matter what good [things] you know [about] people. You must also take into account their reputation, deserved or undeserved. But still, it's sad. If somebody has a very, very bad reputation, you don't give him public responsibility.

I don't think that Nassiri was a bad man. I don't think he was a cruel man. I think he was [pause]. You know many people are lazy, by which I mean they prefer to settle something immediately rather than to think about it and to find other means. Do you know what I mean? He was a military man in the not-so-good sense of the word—a disciplinarian, too strong. But I wouldn't say that he was a cruel man. I don't think he was. I think that again the propaganda against him was terrible.

Public Life of the Security Chief's Wife

HL: When your husband was chief of the Security Organization, was it difficult to be his wife and in the public eye? How did it affect your daily life?

FP: Yes. I'll tell you in what way. Not in the way you think. It was difficult—I'll give you a small example. I was shopping one day at Khiaban-e Manuchehri [Manuchehri Street]. I was a customer at several shops there. A bicycle, a cyclist, went by on the sidewalk and ran into me. I started to bleed. People jumped at him and caught him, and said, "*Khanom*, we will send him to the police." I said, "No. Please let him go."

HL: Did you have bodyguards with you?

FP: No. Never. Never. For heaven's sake! How awful! Never! The shopkeepers said, "*Khanom*, let's take him to the police." I said, "No. Please don't." Then my driver said, "*Khanom*, we must do something." I said, "Please, don't." Anyway, I finished my job and went home. I had a dressing on the wound. It was just a scratch, but it was bleeding freely.

The driver said, "*Khanom*, but why?" I said, "Look here. He was in the wrong, because he was on the sidewalk. He hurt me. He wounded me. But the moment the police learn who he has hurt, then I don't give much for the life of this poor fellow."

In that sense it was very bad. Wherever I went, it was the red carpet [treatment]. I told you about this little welfare society that we wanted to establish, and in the end the whole project was stuck somewhere at the Ministry of the Interior. So I went there with General Stodach. He was chief of staff of the air force. He was retired and of Austrian origin. So we went there, and were very badly received by a fat, big official.

I saw that I really had to do something. I [had not previously] said who I was, [but then] I said, "Well, these regulations of our [charity] have been through all the steps, including through the Security Organization, whose head is my husband, General Pakravan." The man jumped, you know: "Bring some chairs! Bring some tea! *Khanom*, why didn't you tell me?" I said, "Why, does it make any difference? I was the same person a few minutes ago when you received me so badly." I didn't say that, of course. I thought it. I was so mad, you know. I was so mad.

And I remember somebody who [referring to my husband] said, "Yes, His Excellency, in the high position that he occupies." I said, "Please. I stop you right here. Don't make a mistake. My husband never becomes someone because of his position. His position gets some credit because my husband is at the head of it. Do you understand that?" I said, "Whether my husband is at the head of something or not, he'll still be the [same] man he is."

You know. It's funny. I realized that years later. You know the story of Hercules and the stables of the King Augeas that he went to clean? Whenever an organization [acquired] a very bad reputation [for itself], my husband was called to fix it. When it was fixed, he was sent somewhere else. It was the same as chief of G-2. It was the same for the Security Organization. It was the same for the Ministry of Information,[96] [a little] less perhaps.

It was the same for the [Embassy in] Pakistan. The shah said to my husband, "I'm sending you to Pakistan because the Pakistanis complain that we always send [them] second-rate ambassadors. And this is a mission I give to you. You must reestablish our good relations, because Pakistan is very important for us." The same in Paris.[97] You see?

The Charles Jourdan Incident

HL: Years later there was this incident at the Charles Jourdan shoe store in Tehran and Mrs. Parviz Sabeti [interruption].

FP: Yes, I know. I know. I know. That was horrible.

HL: How did you feel when you heard about it?

FP: I was absolutely mad. I was in Iran [at the time]. I was

---

[96] Pakravan was minister of information (1965–66/1344–45).

[97] Pakravan was ambassador to France (1968–72/1347–51).

madder because the man who killed that young man had been our guard when my husband was head of the [Security] Organization. We had two guards. Not at the same time—you know. They were on shifts. His name was Jaffari. Well, Sabeti was the man [about whom my husband said], *moqtaziyat-e zaman*. Remember I told you?[98]

HL: Yes. I do.

FP: And I knew the [people involved]. I mean through other people, I knew this young man was to be married. He accompanied his future mother-in-law and his future wife to the Charles Jourdan [shoe shop] which was not a real Charles Jourdan anyway.

As I was told the story, Madame Sabeti was there. I never met her. If I had, I don't remember her. When you asked me if I had guards wherever I went, she had guards. She chose some shoes. And when she came to pay, she realized that her purse was not in her bag. Her money bag was not there. So she started to make a big to-do, and the shop-owner, knowing who she was, closed all the doors. And he said, "Nobody [pause]." No. No. Not the shopkeeper. This guard came in and said, "Close all doors. We are going to search the people." The future mother-in-law, said, "We have finished our business. We have not stolen anything. We are respectable people. We are going to go out." [The guard] said, "No. You cannot go out." And he stopped them at the door which was a big glass

[98] See p. 26.

pane. And the fiancé saw [the scene] from his car. So, he jumped to rescue his fiancée, and the other [guard] just took out his gun and shot him.

And there were the funerals and the ceremonies, you know. The woman was so sorry [that] she wanted to go and attend [the memorial service]. Stupid woman.

HL: Mrs. Sabeti?

FP: Yes. And they told her, "*Khanom.* Come if you want. But if you come, you must know you will be torn to pieces."

What shocked me even more was that they arrested Jaffari, the man who shot the young man. You see? Whereas he wasn't responsible. He was given a gun and [told], "You guard Madame Sabeti. If anything happens to her, you shoot." That's right. It was as plain as that. Otherwise, he wouldn't have shot [him]. Why [didn't] he ever shoot anybody when he was in my house. He didn't even have a gun, I believe.

That [incident] was one of the things you must put as one of the causes of the Iranian revolution. I was so mad. I told my husband, I said, "Go and see the shah. Please go and see him. Tell him that the whole truth must be told. Sabeti must be arrested, and his wife, and the shop-owner, everybody. And this man [Jaffari], of course, because he obeyed, was just a pawn." I said, "You must. The whole town knows the truth. Why hide it?"

I was very mad, I must say. I was so mad that when a dinner party was arranged at the Foreign Affairs Club—the fantastic club [built] by the Ministry of Foreign Affairs in the Dezashib [district]—and I saw the [guest] list and I told the host, "If you sit me next to Sabeti, I will never speak to you again." And I turned my back. I was never sitting beside him. I was sitting away, and whenever he addressed me, I showed him my shoulder.

HL: Did General Pakravan speak to the shah about this incident?

FP: I don't remember. I know that he also was very, very mad. Perhaps he did. Perhaps he did. I don't know. It was a time when I [pause]. No. No. No. He was in hospital. That's right. I didn't say that to him. It was when he had his heart attack. I don't remember exactly the dates. No. No. No.

Appointment to the Ministry of Court

HL: When you returned from France, what post was given to your husband?

FP: Well, you know. There were many rumors when he was in France. First of all, people said that according to the regulations of the Ministry of Foreign Affairs, a man is nominated for four years. He can have an additional year in another place which is stupid because you don't nominate someone as ambassador for one year.

So, we had already two years—three years in Pakistan when the shah insisted that he wanted Hassan [to go to Paris]. [In the meantime] Hoveida [had] said [to me], "You know, I keep on asking His Majesty to make Hassan minister and he refuses. He says, 'I need him.' I tell His Majesty I need Pakravan and [His Majesty] says, 'I need him even more.'" Fortunately, I don't know how true it is.

Anyway, the shah insisted that my husband should become ambassador in Paris. But, we thought it was for only two years according to the regulations. But [the shah] told Ardeshir Zahedi[99] (and Ardeshir Zahedi told me this himself), "I don't know. You manage with your regulations. I want Pakravan to stay the whole four years in Paris." So, we stayed the whole four years in Paris—even a little bit more, a few days more.

But the rumors started immediately: "Ah, you know. Your husband is being recalled." I said, "Look here. My husband should have been in Paris [for only] two years. It's been four years [now]." And my husband always said you had to respect regulations. [Otherwise] what was the point of having them?

So, they started to [say], "Ah, you know. Your husband will be recalled because he's going to be made prime minister." This sort of thing. "He's going to be recalled to be made minister of foreign affairs." I had prepared a reply. I [would] say, "Look here. My husband is an army man, although retired. So, a general is supposed to prepare [for] war, or at least to

---

[99] Ardeshir Zahedi, son of General Fazlollah Zahedi, former son-in-law of Mohammad-Reza Shah, ambassador to the United States (1960–62/1339–41), ambassador to the United Kingdom (1962–67/1341–46), foreign minister (1967–71/1346–50), and ambassador to the United States (1972–79/1351–57).

prevent war. The minister of foreign affairs is supposed to make peace between [countries]. So, how can you have an army man at the head of the foreign ministry?" [I would say] things like that to try to make people stop their stupid rumors.

Anyway, my husband thought that he had been in public service for years. He thought he would retire and retire in Paris because he liked France very much. Then he had to go back to Iran to settle [his affairs]. I mean, he couldn't just say good-bye. He had to go and see the shah, make his final report, and all that. And we had a piece of land there and he said, "You know, I would like to build this house."

And the shah [pause]. Everybody thought that he would be made at least senator. [Instead] he received the job of that famous Boushehri I told you about. It was *moshaver-e alli-ye darbar* [مـشـاور عـالی دربار], senior counselor of the Ministry of Court].

My husband just hated the job, because he had the feeling that he could be so useful. And [this position] was just a job to get a salary and nothing else. So he asked to have his office somewhere downtown, because he couldn't stand these comings and goings in the court and all this gossiping and all that.

And then he had his heart attack. Here I must say when the trouble started in Iran in the summer of 1978 [1357], now and then somebody would telephone our house or his office and [implore him], "Please, General, go and say this, and this, and this to the shah." Or they [would] come to our house [and say], "Please, you must go to the shah. You are the only person to whom he will listen." And my husband would say, "No. No. No. No. The shah doesn't see me. He never receives me. I am quite put aside."

So one day, I told him, "Why do you say such things? First of all, it's undignified because we live in Persian society. If you say that you are out of favor, people will add to it and say that you've been kicked out. And secondly, you haven't tried. Ask for an audience. If he refuses, okay, then you'll resign and we'll go back to Paris." It's funny, that in some cases he was very shy.

Pakravan's Audiences with the Shah

So he asked for an audience, and the shah immediately agreed. He stayed quite a long time, and when he came back [home], he was so upset, so moved. He wasn't a man to show his feelings. He had very, very good control of himself. He said, "I've never been so touched in my life. You know, I've been working with the shah closely since both of us were young men. This is the first time he asked me personal questions that he never [had before]. He asked about you and all the children by name. He made personal remarks—he never did that [before]." [My husband continued], "You know, I think he likes me quite well." I said, "Of course he likes you."

The really important thing he told [the shah was the following]: On a trip to Kashan, we had to cross the famous south of Tehran. I couldn't believe my eyes! I just couldn't believe my eyes—the conditions in which people lived! It was incredible! Some of them lived in pens, completely patched up with pieces of nylon on them. The open-air canals were heaped with dirt and garbage. The water was black and smelly. You could not imagine what it was [like]. You cannot visualize that.

HL: When was the last time you had seen this part of Tehran?

FP: In the 1970s [1350s], I think. Well, I wasn't in Tehran for many years, you know. I had predicted right. I said that it would go from bad to worse. It was in 1976 or 1977 [1355 or 1356] that we went on this trip to Natanz and Kashan. Anyway, the important thing is that we were terribly worried.

[During his audience with the shah], my husband [referring to conditions in south Tehran] told him, "You know, this is how the people live there. If you're not going to do something immediately from a human point of view, do it for your own safety, because this is a powder keg. Two million people living like that—your capital city is going to explode and we'll all be swept by the explosion." Then the next day, he showed photographs to the queen. It was too late, too late, too late. There is a book written by Alan Paton called *Too Late the Phalarope*. The phalarope is a South African bird.

After that [audience], the shah saw my husband very often. This is when he said, "Whenever, I see the shah, I have the impression that he is like a drowning man who sees me as some safety to which to cling."

One day, he said, "[The shah] is completely flattened." (We always spoke French.) *"Aplati"* [crushed is] what he said. "What do you mean?" I asked. He said, "One day [the shah] says, 'I'm going all the way toward democracy. I'm going to give total freedom. I think we've made a terrible mistake. We'll have free elections. We'll have a free press. We'll have freedom of expression—freedom of everything, criticism and everything. It's time to have it.' The next day he [would] be completely crushed." The shah knew about the criticism. He knew about the grudge [of the people]. He knew about everything. The only thing that really killed him was the hatred [of the people], because [only] a few weeks before [he thought that] he was loved and that people looked up to him.

The Last Days of the Monarchy

So the last measure to save the house was to nominate my husband [to be] in complete charge of all the administration and finances of the Ministry of Court.

HL: Was this during Hoveida's or Ardalan's[100] tenure at

---

[100] Ali-Gholi Ardalan, official of the Ministry of Foreign Affairs, special assistant to the prime minister (1942/1321), acting minister of foreign affairs (1950/1329), minister of state (1955/1334), minister of industries and mines (1955–56/1334–35), minister of foreign affairs (1956–57/1335–36 and 1957–58/1336–37), and minister of court (1978–79/1357). He had also served as ambassador to the United States and the Soviet Union.

Memoirs of Fatemeh Pakravan

the Ministry of Court?

FP: No. No. Hoveida wasn't [there]. It was Ali-Gholi Ardalan. And [my husband] was mad, he didn't like it. He said, "I'm finishing my career as chief accountant of [the court]." I said, "Darling, you're not the chief accountant." They always used my husband for his good name.

HL: Why did he accept this position?

FP: It was his sense of service. He said, "Poor Ardalan. I cannot drop him. Poor old man." And everybody congratulated him, because they thought he was—he's become [pause].

People are so stupid. All these ranks and positions—he didn't care about that. One day he came [home] absolutely mad. He [had] said to the king, "You know, Majesty, I don't want any interference [from others]." [He said this] because there were several families since the time of the late shah, the other shah, who had a strong hold over all the activities of the [court]. So much so that one day he came back from the office and said, "You know, we don't have one shah." I said, "What do you mean?" He said, "We have at least twelve of them. And the weakest is the one who wears the crown!"

HL: The "weakest?"

FP: The "weakest." That's what my husband said. I'll never forget it. Because several families were traditionally in the court. They really did exactly as they wished.

HL: You mean, the [shah's] sisters and brothers?

FP: No. No. No. The officials.

HL: Really?

FP: Yes, like the Behbahanis.[101] People like that. They would never give up. And my husband had to fight, [something] he hated. The order was that no expense in the court, no kind of project or anything, could go directly to the shah. [They had to] go through my husband. [They wanted him] to agree to something fantastic. He said, "You know, they are renovating, I don't know what, for 30 million tomans." I said, "But why?" He said, "How can I refuse it now? It's almost finished and the man must be paid." But this situation that we had [was] sheer madness. Behbahanian still went over his head to the minister of court to approve some projects. And my husband was very, very mad.

And in the end when [I was in Paris and he was in Tehran], I told him over the phone, "Darling, you know Khomeini is coming back.[102] Please, please leave! Leave, leave!" He said, "How can I leave? All these people at the court have nobody but Ardalan and me." And by these [people] he meant the drivers, the gardeners, the cooks, the bakers, all this small population of the court who were left high and dry without a pension, without any future—in danger perhaps. So he stayed.

HL: You were in Paris in February of 1979 [Bahman 1357]?

FP: Yes. When I telephoned him, I was here. He took me

---

[101] Reference is to Mohammad-Jafar Behbahanian, chief of financial affairs of the royal family.

[102] Ayatollah Rouhollah Khomeini returned to Tehran on 1 February 1979 (12 Bahman 1357).

to Paris. I told you. He insisted that I should go to Paris to be with the children, and I refused. I said, "No. I will never leave you." And he pretended that he had to see his heart specialist, because he was taking fifteen of these heart pills, you know. So he brought me [to Paris and in order to allay] suspicion, he bought me a return [round trip] ticket. So we came to Paris, and stayed for ten days, and then he went [back to Tehran]. That was the last time I saw him.

HL: When was this? November?

FP: November of 1978—21st of November of 1978 [30 Azar 1357]. We arrived here on the 12th [21 Azar] and on the 21st [30 Azar] he went back and [pause]

Arrest of Amir-Abbas Hoveida

HL: What are your recollections regarding the arrest of Prime Minister Hoveida?

FP: While I was in Tehran—that is something historical—there was a man from France Inter[103] who telephoned all the time. I didn't know he was telephoning from Paris. And he kept on ringing. [One day he called and said], "I want to speak to His Excellency." I said, "Well, he's not here." My husband had left in the morning and then his driver—his official driver—came home and had a snack. I asked "Where is *timsar*?" He said, "He's at the court. I have to go back there." [It took a long time for my husband to come home that day.] He came

---

[103] A French radio and television news program.

back at eight o'clock.

And the man telephoned again, [when] we were having dinner. [On the phone] my husband laughed and said, "No. No. No. Monsieur Yves Vincent. I am nothing. I'm nothing at all. You ask the prime minister. You ask the minister of foreign affairs. I am just the accountant of the court." And he laughed and laughed. I asked, "Why do you say that?" He said, "Because I don't like this job. After I settle everything, I will resign. It's ridiculous. I am an officer. I am a soldier." That surprised me.

He said, "You know, of all the positions I [have] held in my life, the only one I am proud of is to [have been] a soldier." I said, "Really? But you didn't become an officer out of conviction. You became [one], because your father wanted you to." He said, "Yes, but I think there is great honor in being a soldier."

So I said, "What's the matter? What happened [today]?" He said, "Oh, you don't know. We had a meeting with several people and the queen. She's a lioness, that woman. She wants to see all kinds of measures—and do this and that—to stop this nonsense of the subversion." One of the measures taken, he said, was the arrest of Hoveida. I said, "And so?" He said, "I was against it."

HL: This was a meeting with the queen, without the participation of the shah?

FP: Yes. The shah was in his [own] office. One of the men who [met with the queen] was Seyyed Mehdi Pirasteh.[104] He

Memoirs of Fatemeh Pakravan

came to see me before he left for—I don't know where.

HL: Canada.

FP: Canada, I think. He said, "Whenever we used to go to the office of the shah, I [would] stand on the threshold [of the room] and say, 'Majesty, we don't enter your office, because we are afraid of your ire. So we want to have a way to rush back.'" And the shah was very, very upset. I don't know who decided on that [Hoveida's arrest], [but], my husband was very upset. [At the end of the meeting, the shah], had asked, "All right. Do you think [the arrest of Hoveida] is necessary?"

HL: Who asked this? The shah?

FP: The shah. There was an army officer, General Oveisi,[105] who responded, "Majesty, *az nan-e shab vajeb-tar ast* [از نان شب واجب تر است]. It is more essential than the evening's bread]."

HL: Could he have been General Nasser Moghadam?[106]

---

[104] Seyyed Mehdi Pirasteh was the son of Haji Motamed (a cleric and landowner). Pirasteh received his university education in law and politics. His posts included: public prosecutor (1949/1328), Sixteenth and Eighteenth Majles deputy from Saveh and Zarand, provincial governor, and minister of the interior (1963–64/1342–43). See his memoirs in the Harvard Iranian Oral History Collection.

[105] General Gholam-Ali Oveisi, one of Iran's four-star generals, [arteshbod, ارتشبد] commander of the imperial guards, commander of the gendarmerie (1965–72/1344–51), commander of the army (1972–78/1351–57), military governor of Tehran (1978/1357), and acting minister of labor and social affairs (1978/1357). He was assassinated in Paris (1981/1360[?]).

[106] General Nasser Moghadam, chief of military intelligence (G-2), deputy prime minister and director of State Intelligence and Security

FP: No. I think it was Oveisi. And the shah said, "All right," because Hoveida was universally hated, you know. He was hated. It was fantastic. My husband and Hoveida knew each other since they were children.

And the shah said, "All right. Then let General Pakravan tell him that he's [being] arrested." My husband said, "Never! I will never do that. I am against it. I will never do it." The shah was very courageous. He took the phone and telephoned Hoveida himself.[107]

HL: Really?

FP: "It has been decided by a committee here in the palace that you are to be arrested," the shah said, and Hoveida replied, "All right. Arrest me."

Hoveida was very fond of my husband. I think he was the only person he trusted, really, because he said many, many things to my husband that he wouldn't say to anybody else. Later on, a senator who was in prison with my husband told me, "Hoveida used to send books in French to your husband." Very often they spoke, when nobody was there. They spoke in French. When the books stopped coming, they guessed that [Hoveida] must have been liquidated.

Hoveida was arrested under the shah. And [on the eve of

Organization (1978–79/1357), and acting minister of energy (1978–79/1357). He was executed by the revolutionary court in 1979/1357.

[107] For more information regarding this telephone conversation see *Memoirs of Abdolmadjid Madjidi* (Cambridge, Mass.: Harvard Center for Middle Eastern Studies, 1998), p. 209.

the Revolution] when they emptied the prisons, he was left all alone. Everybody knows that he telephoned the authorities, saying, "Here I am." He never thought of [escaping].[108] He was a very interesting personality.

My daughter worked for him for three years as [his] personal secretary. My sister knew him very well. I think in a way he was a great man, because he didn't pay any attention to anything. He said, "Why should I have the humiliation of hiding myself or of running away?" My husband had the same mentality.

Some people who worked in the Ministry of Information, *Ershad-e Melli* [ارشاد ملی, National Guidance], had seen the list [of those to be arrested] with my husband's name [on it]. They came and begged him to come to their houses or to go somewhere [and hide]. He said, "No." Alavi-Kia must have told you. He told Alavi-Kia, "Take your wife and children and go away from here." [Alavi-Kia had] said, *"Timsar*, what about you?" He said, "I must stay here even though I [may be] killed, even at the cost of my life." He would never flee. Never, never, never.

Arrest of General Pakravan

HL: When did they seize your husband?

FP: Well, I think I told you when we started [the interview]

---

[108] For details of Hoveida's decision to hand himself over to the revolutionary forces see Dr. Fereshte Ensha's memoirs contained in the Harvard Iranian Oral History Collection and available to researchers as of the year 2002/1381.

that Khomeini is an unforgiving man—the more he owes someone, the more he hates him. And he owed everything to my husband: his title of Ayatollah, his life, his good treatment when he was arrested—everything.[109]

Now of course the rumor—but I don't want. I want to say exactly what we know. What my son tells me. What my son-in-law, Naderzad [has told me]. The young people were very fond of my husband, and he understood them very well. So that Friday, the 16th of February 1979 [27 Bahman 1357], he took some friends to our house for lunch, and they had a wonderful time. (My son was not there.) Then at 3:30 [P.M.] my husband told them, "I want to rest, please." After his heart attack, [he] tired easily. So they went.

At five o'clock he got up to go to the kitchen to get a glass of water. There was lots of noise outside—shouting and all that. He said to our servant, "What's the matter?" This young man came back pale and said, "*Timsar*, they've come to take you away."

[The servant related the story to me later]. He said, "You know, His Excellency took the glass [of water]. He never took the trouble to put on shoes, and walked out with his slippers. When the [arresting agents] saw him, they were so full of respect." [The servant] wanted to console me, poor man: "They were so respectful. They bowed to him. They opened the door." And he said, "I ran after the car, because it was the end of

---
[109] See p. 39.

winter, very cold, and he had gone without a coat or anything."
I asked, "And then what happened?" He said, "Well, they
stopped the car and took his coat to him. And I was crying."
[My husband] didn't say a word. They took him to a
committee at Kashanak[110] and from there to Madraseh-e Alavi
[مدرسه علوى, the Alavi School].[111]

When my son came back, he was told that his father had
been arrested. He immediately rushed to his brother-in-law,
and they tried every place. They [were told], "We don't know.
Go to the Alavi School." They went there. They took some
clothes and his medicine. And the man in charge refused it,
and said, "No. No. We have everything for him. Besides, he's
not arrested at all. Who said he was arrested? He is the guest
of the ayatollah. We want to ask him a few questions about the
court, not about the time when he was head of security or
ambassador, or minister of information, or anything. It's a
matter of a few days." You see how clever!

But then, I told you, this cousin of Hoveida[112] saw him.
They blindfolded him and took him on the steps. And then all
the lies started. My son told me, "There is a very nice guard
there. He brings me little notes from my father. He says that
Daddy is not in prison, but in the infirmary. He's on a nice bed

---

[110] A village north of Tehran near the Niavaran Palace.

[111] A secondary school with a heavy emphasis on Islamic studies.
It was used as the headquarters of the revolution during its first days.

[112] Dr. Fereshte Ensha. See her memoirs in the Harvard Iranian
Oral History Collection.

and he looks after him. He brings the barber every other day. He washes his clothes. He gives him very good food, and the doctor is always there in attendance."

My husband used to write little notes and this fellow would bring [them to] my son and give them [to him]. Rendezvous in very, very complicated places—at such-and-such place, you know. And he would insist that he tear [up] the little notes, so we don't have anything from my husband. Every time, my husband would say, "Give him 500 tomans. Give him [pause]. He's very nice to me."

But actually, I heard from the senator who was with [my husband in prison], who said, "It wasn't at all like that. He wasn't at all. After a few days, he was straightaway put into prison with no mattress, no bedding, nothing." You remember seeing images, photos, of Hoveida. But he was at least on a mattress. My husband was on the floor. It was the Red Cross, the International Red Cross, that after a month obliged them to give bedding to the prisoners.

I asked, "But who was this nice man?" He said, "Oh well. There was a man to whom we used to give money. He was a little better than the others. We used to give him money to buy books for us. And he refused. He brought us religious books. But your husband wanted *Masnavi*."[113] It's funny, because my husband was never interested in poetry, even in French poetry.

---

[113] *Masnavi* is the title of a six-volume poetic work by Jalal al-Din Mohammad Balkhi, known as Mowlana.

Then the senator told me that [my husband] asked him to teach him Turkish, because the senator was from Azerbaijan, and also to read poetry to him, especially *Masnavi*. And he said, "[Your husband] told me, 'Read me a part and at nine o'clock every night, ask me to recite it to you.'" And [the senator] said, "He recited it perfectly."

Then he did something which I never told anybody. He went on a hunger strike. He told this senator who was showing him the photos of his wife and his children, "Are you very fond of them?" The senator said, "Yes." He said, "Are you going to swear to keep secret what I'm going to tell you? I have to tell you something." The senator told me, "You know, I had never met your husband. I said [to myself], 'My God, it's true. He has a very, very good reputation, but still he was head of SAVAK. Perhaps he did something he wants to confess to me.'" [My husband] said, "Okay. I'm going to go on a hunger strike, but I don't want it to be known. It's not as a protest. It's as a discipline. I know the world championship was 49 or 45 days. I want to see if I can break it."

So, he went on for 35 days, [taking] nothing, but water and tea without sugar. [The senator] said, "One day I put sugar in his tea. He refused it." This surprises me, because my husband liked tea and coffee very, very sweet. He said, "And you know, he was fantastic. He was a hero. He was a saint. He's a martyr. But he is a saint." I said, "How come?" He said, "He was so detached. He had reached such a high spiritual level. I was amazed."

He said, "One day he smiled and said, 'It's funny. I've never lived in such conditions even in the army, in such complete *dénuement* [destitution]. No kind of material comfort at all, the worst possible material conditions. I know what's going to happen to me. It will be the machine gun, but I've never felt so well.' He said, 'I've not been eating for 35 days and I feel perfectly well.'" But he started to smoke which [meant] that he knew he was going to be condemned.

They never allowed my son to see him, because they said inquiries were going on. It wasn't true. Somehow all the secrets come out. The interrogator told somebody, who told my son, that when they opened his file—his so-called file—there was only one piece of paper. And that was the testimony of a young man, who had been arrested under my husband and who [had given] testimony to the humane treatment he had [received] and that General Pakravan had him released very [quickly].

So he knew. And [the senator] said, "Three days later was his execution. He was taken from my cell and I never heard of him [again]."

Now, any other questions?

Appendix 1
List of Narrators

Abadian, Bahman, Plan Organization deputy director

Abbas-Attaie, Ramzi (Adm.), navy commander

Adamiyatt, Tahmouress, ambassador to the Soviet Union

Adl-Naficy, Ozma, director general, Ministry of Labor

Afshar-Ghassemlou, Amir-Khosrow, minister of foreign affairs

Aghayan, Felix, senator

Aghayan, Shahin, lawyer

al-Musawi-Esfahani, Musa, grandson of Ayatollah Abolhassan Esfahani, Shiite leader

Alamouti, Mostafa, journalist and Majles deputy

Alavi-Kia, Hassan (Gen.), deputy chief of SAVAK

Alikhani, Alinaghi, minister of economy

Amini, Ali, prime minister

Amini, Nosratollah, Mossadegh lawyer and mayor of Tehran

Amirazizi, Sadegh (Gen.), minister of the interior

Amirkeivan, Amir, labor leader

Amirteymour, Mohammad-Ebrahim, minister of labor

Ashtiani, Mohammad-Reza, Majles deputy

Azar, Mehdi (Dr.), minister of education

Harvard Iranian Oral History Collection

Azmoudeh, Hossein (Gen.), prosecutor, Mossadegh trial

Azod-Qajar, Abounasr, businessman and vice president, Iran Chamber of Commerce, industries, and Mines

Baghaie-Kermani, Mozaffar, Majles deputy and Toilers Party leader

Baheri, Mohammad, minister of justice

Bakhtiar, Shapour, prime minister

Baniahmad, Ahmad, Majles deputy

Banisadr, Abolhassan, president of Islamic Republic of Iran

Behnia, Abolhassan, minister of roads

Boroumand, Abdolrahman, businessman and political activist

Daftari, Mohammad (Gen.), national police chief

Derakhshesh, Mohammad, minister of education

Djafroudi, Kazem, senator

Djam, Fereydoun, chief of Supreme Commander's Staff

Dolatshahi, Mehrangiz, Majles deputy and ambassador

Ebtehaj, Abolhassan, Plan Organization director[114]

Eghbal, Khosro, lawyer

Ensha, Fereshte (Dr.), physician and Premier Hoveida niece

Fardoust, Tala, wife of SAVAK deputy director

Farivar, Gholam-Ali, Iran Party leader

---

[114] See Ali-Reza Arouzi, ed., *Khaterat-e Abolhassan Ebtehaj* (Memoirs of Abolhassan Ebtehaj), 2 vols. (London: Abolhassan Ebtehaj, 1370). A major portion of this book is based on the transcript of thirty-two hours of interview conducted by the Harvard Iranian Oral History Project with Mr. Ebtehaj.

Farmanfarmaian, Khodadad, Plan Organization director

Fartash, Abbas (Gen.), Imperial Guards

Firouz, Mozaffar, minister of labor and propaganda

Firouz, Safiyeh Nemazee, leader of women's movement

Foroughi, Mahmoud, ambassador to Washington

Frye, Richard N., Harvard University professor and head of Asia Institute, Pahlavi University

Gharib, Hormoz, chief of protocol, Ministry of Court

Ghashghaie, Mohammad-Nasser, tribal chief and senator

Ghoreishi, Ahmad, National University chancellor

Habibolahi, Kamal (Adm.), navy commander

Hadjiseyd-Djavadi, Ali-Asghar, writer

Hairi-Yazdi, Mehdi, professor of theology and son of Ayatollah Abdolkarim Hairi, Shiite leader

Harney, Desmond, British diplomat

Hashemi, Manouchehr (Gen.), SAVAK counterespionage

Hasheminejad, Mohsen (Gen.), Imperial Guards commander

Hezarkhani, Manouchehr (Dr.), political activist

Homayoun, Daryoush, minister of information

Homayouni, Fazlollah (Gen.), army commander in Kurdistan

Izadi, Ali, chief of Princess Ashraf's secretariat

Jazayeri, Shamseddin, minister of education

Kadjar, Hamid (Prince), son of last Qajar crown prince

Kalali, Manouchehr, secretary-general, Iran Novin Party

Harvard Iranian Oral History Collection

Kamrooz-Atabai, Badry, head of Royal Library

Kashani, Kamran, professor, Center for Management Studies

Katouzian, Homayoun, university professor

Kechavarz, Fereydoun (Dr.), minister of education and Tudeh leader

Khanlary, Moloud, political activist

Kheradjou, Abolghasem, managing director, Industrial and Mining Development Bank of Iran

Khorsandi, Hadi, satirist and publisher of *Asghar Agha*

Khosrovani, Ataollah, minister of labor

Khosrovani, Parviz (Gen.), head of Tehran gendarmerie

Kia, Haj-Ali, head of military intelligence

Ladjevardi, Ghassem, businessman and senator

Ladjevardian, Akbar, businessman and vice president, Tehran Chamber of Commerce

Lahidji, Abdolkarim, lawyer and human rights activist

Lankarani, Mostafa, Tudeh Party

Lebaschi, Abolghassem, bazaar representative, National Front

Madani, Ahmad (Adm.), navy commander

Madjidi, Abdolmadjid, Plan Organization director

Mahdavi, Ebrahim, minister of agriculture

Mahdavi, Fereidoun, deputy secretary-gen, Rastakhiz Party

Mahfoozi, Ali-Reza, Cherik-ha-ye Fadaii-e Khalq

Mahvi, Abolfath, businessman and advisor to the shah

Malek, Hossein, writer

Matine-Daftary, Hedayat, lawyer and National Democratic Front leader

Maybud (Mehbod), Ahmed, diplomat and advisor to the shah

Mehr, Farhang, Pahlavi University chancellor

Middleton, George, British chargé d'affaires

Miller, William, American diplomat

Mina, Parviz, National Iranian Oil Company director

Minbashian, Fathollah, army commander

Mirfendereski, Ahmad, minister of foreign affairs

Mirzazadeh, Nemat, poet

Mobasheri, Asadollah, minister of justice

Mobasser, Mohsen (Gen.), national police chief

Modjtahedi, Mohammad-Ali, Alborz High School principal

Moghadam, Gholam-Reza, Central Bank deputy governor

Moghaddam-Maraghehi, Rahmatollah, Radical Party leader

Mohtadi, Ali-Akbar (Col.), aide to Premier Razmara

Mossadegh, Gholam-Hossein, physician and aide to father

Motameni, Mehdi, treasurer, Iran Chamber of Commerce, industries, and Mines

Naficy, Habib, vice minister of labor

Nahavandi, Houshang, Tehran University chancellor

Nategh, Homa, historian

Nazih, Hassan, Bar Association president

Pakdaman, Nasser, Tehran University professor

Pakravan, Fatemeh, wife of Gen. Hassan Pakravan, chief of the State Intelligence and Security Organization, cabinet minister and diplomat.

Pedram, Mohammad, diplomat

Pejman, Issa (Col.), SAVAK director-general

Pezechgpour, Mohsen, Pan-Iranist Party leader

Pichdad, Amir (Dr.), Socialist League activist

Pirasteh, Mehdi, minister of the interior

Rajaie-Khorasani, Said, IRI ambassador to the UN

Rajavi, Massoud, Mojahedin-e Khalq leader

Rambod, Holakou, minister of state

Ramsbotham, Peter (Sir), British ambassador

Rockwell, Stewart, American chargé d'affaires

Rohani, Parvin, wife of minister of agriculture

Saedi, Gholam-Hossein (Dr.), playwright[115]

Salamatian, Ahmad, vice minister of foreign affairs

Samii, Mehdi, Central Bank governor

Sanjabi, Karim, National Front leader[116]

Shakeri, Khosrow, scholar

---

[115] His memoirs were published in full after his death in November 1985 (Mehr 1364) by his wife in the last issue of *Alefba*.

[116] See Karim Sanjabi, *Omid-ha va Na-omidi-ha: Khaterat-e Doctor Karim Sanjabi* (London: Jebheh Melliyoun Iran, 1367). The content of this book is based wholly on transcript of thirty-three hours of interview conducted by the Harvard Iranian Oral History Project with Mr. Sanjabi.

Shanehchi, Mohammad, Ayatollah Taleghani aide

Sharif-Emami, Jafar, prime minister

Tehrani, Mehdi, opposition figure

Toufanian, Hassan (Gen.), military procurement head

Wright, Denis (Sir), British ambassador

Yeganeh, Mohammad, minister of economic affairs and finance

Zahedi, Ardeshir, minister of foreign affairs

Zarghamee, Mehdi, Aryamehr University chancellor

Zirakzadeh, Ahmad, National Front leader

Names of a number of narrators have been withheld to protect their identity.

Harvard Iranian Oral History Collection

Appendix 2
Project Staff

Staff Members

Shahin Bassiri, transcriber

Emma Dolkhanian, transcriber

Margaret DuBois, staff assistant

Parouchestia Goodarzi, research assistant

Layegheh Hodaii (Doorandish), transcriber

Habib Ladjevardi, project director

Zia Sedghi, processing supervisor, interviewer and translator

Laura Serafin, staff assistant

Interviewers

Shahla Haeri

Shahrokh Meskoob

John Mojdehi

Appendix 3
Libraries Holding the Collection

Transcripts and Tape Recordings
Harvard University
Houghton Library
Cambridge, MA 02138

University of Oxford
Department of Oriental Books
Bodleian Library
Broad Street
Oxford OX1 3BG, England

Microfiche Only
Bibliothèque Nationale
2, rue Vivienne
75084 Paris Cedex 02, France

The John Rylands University Library
University of Manchester
Oxford Road
Manchester, England

Library of Congress
Middle East Section
Washington, DC 20540

New York University
E. H. Bobst Library
70 Washington Square South
New York, NY 10012

Harvard Iranian Oral History Collection

School of Oriental and African Studies
University of London
Russell Square
London, England

University of Bamberg
Postfach 1549
D-8600 Bamberg, Germany

University of British Columbia
Humanities and Social Sciences Division
Main Library
Vancouver, BC, Canada

University of California, San Diego
Social Sciences and Humanities Library
University Library Building 0175R
La Jolla, California 92093-0175

University of Chicago
Middle East Department
Rengenstein Library
1100 East 57th Street
Chicago, IL 60637

University of Tübingen
Wilhemstrasse 32
Postfach 2620
D 7400 Tübingen 1, Germany

Index

A
Adl, Parviz ... 88
Adl, Yahya (Dr.) ... 72, 75
Afshars ... 57
agrarian reform ... 28, 30-31
air force ... 15, 58, 113
Ala, Hossein ... 98-99, 105
Alam, Amir-Asadollah ... 40, 64-65
Alam, Iran (Dr.) ... 79
Alam, Touran (Dr.) ... 79
Alavi-Kia, Hassan (Gen.) ... 20, 110, 129
Alexandria, Egypt ... 17
Allies ... 54, 60
America ... 16, 28, 35, 38, 43, 47, 53-4, 109
American School ... 71
Amiralam, Amirkeivan (Alam al-Dowleh)) ... 79
Anzac ... 54
Ardalan, Ali-Gholi ... 122-124
Armenians ... 36, 52, 60-61
army ... 15, 17-19, 24, 32-34, 53, 118, 127, 134
Army General Staff ... 80
army chief of staff ... 103
Ashtiani Javad (Dr.) ... 52
Australia ... 54
Austrian ... 53, 113
Azerbaijan ... 15, 56, 133

B
Baharmast, Mahmoud (Gen.) ... 17
Bakhtiar, Teymour (Gen.) ... 21-24
Bakhtiari family ... 28
Bank Melli Hospital ... 54
Behbahanian, Mohammad-Jafar ... 124
Behjatabad ... 60-62
Birjand ... 64

Bombay 82-83, 85
Bonnier, Henri 48-49
de Borchgrave, Arnaud 109
Boushehri-Dehdashti, Javad (Amirhomayoun) 95, 119
Boushehri, Mehdi 91
British 28, 54
British ambassador 89
Buckingham Palace 83
Bushehr 28

C

Cadet Academy 18
Cairo 17, 48
CENTO 23, 35
Chafik, Shahryar (Prince) 91-92
Cherik-ha-ye Fadaii-e Khalq-e Iran, Sazman-e 106
CIA 18
Cinema Rex, Abadan 38
communists 15, 74
court of England 90
Court, Ministry of 41, 99, 119, 123
court, the imperial .. 47, 49, 54, 81, 85, 87, 89, 91, 96, 99, 119, 123-26, 131

D

defense, minister of 14
Delhi 63, 82-83
democracy 26, 108, 122
Democrat Party of Iran 74
Development and Housing, Ministry of 29
Dezashib district of Tehran 117
dictatorship 108

E

earthquake in the Qazvin area 28
Ebtehaj, Gholam-Hossein 57
Eghbal, Manouchehr (Dr.) 100-103, 105
Egypt 17

Elysée Palace 88
Esfahan 61
Esfandiary, Soraya (former queen) 81-85
Europe 17, 24, 35, 73
Evans, Courtney (Dr.) 22

F
Falsafi, Mohammad-Taghi (Sheikh) 30
Fardoust, Hossein (Gen.) 110
Farifteh, Djavad 16, 50-52, 55
Firouz, Mozaffar 74-75
Fontaine, André 19
Fontainebleau, France 18
Foreign Affairs, Ministry of 118-119, 126
Foroughi, Mohsen 66
France 13, 16, 50-51, 53, 55, 57, 63, 94, 107, 109, 117, 119
France Inter 125
Franco-Iranian Association 88
French army 17
French embassy 102
French General Staff 16-17
French language .. 46, 51-53, 57-58, 69, 93, 97, 102, 122, 128, 132

G
G-2, see military intelligence
gendarmerie 15
Germany 54, 110
Gharagozlou, Mary 28, 31
Ghavam, Ahmad (Ghavam al-Saltaneh) 79-80
Ghomi, Hassan (Ayatollah) 40
Golestan Palace 66
Gurkhas 54

H
Hamadan 28
handicrafts 65
Health, Ministry of 52

Harvard Iranian Oral History Collection

Helleu, Madame 88
von Herzfeld, Stephan 53
Hoveida, Amir-Abbas   45-46, 117, 122-123, 125-128, 131-132

I
Imam Hossein 45
India 19-20, 54, 58, 63, 82, 109
Information, Ministry of 45-46, 67-68, 114, 129, 131
Institute for Foreign Languages 58
International Red Cross 55, 132
Iran Tour Company 64
Italy 55

J
Jaffari (SAVAK body guard) 115-116
Jahanbani. Massoud 88
Jordan 109

K
Kashan 120-21
Kechavarz, Fereydoun (Dr.) 74
Khalkhali, Sadegh (Sheikh) 41
Khomeini, Rouhollah (Ayatollah) 29-30, 32, 35-43, 48, 59, 87, 96, 124, 130
Khorasan 55-56, 64
Kia, Haj-Ali (Gen.) 24
Kurdistan 15, 44

L
Lebanon 109
Liège, Belgium 17
Loghman-Adham, Hossein 47, 89
Lycée français, Cairo 17

M
Majles 44, 65, 73
Mansour, Hassan-Ali 44-45, 65, 101-106
Mao Tse-tung 69, 109

Margaret (Princess) 89
Marquis of Cuernavaca 53
martial law 14, 43
Mashhad 32, 55
Maximilian 53
Mexico 48, 53
military intelligence (G-2) 14, 24, 28, 80-81, 87, 114
Moaven, Hossein (Dr.) 72-73
Mojahedin Khalgh-e Iran, Sazman-e 106, 108, 110
Mossadegh, Gholam-Hossein (Dr.) 15, 17, 52
Mossadegh, Mohammad 13-17, 31, 52, 54, 59, 69-73, 75-78, 81, 87, 92, 106
Mossadegh, Najm al-Saltaneh 72, 77
Mossadegh, Zia al-Saltaneh 70
mullahs 31-32, 34, 39, 41-42
Muslim Brotherhood 104

N
Naderzad, Jahangir 130
Nafisi, Ahmad 63
Nahavandi, Houshang 29
Najmiyeh Foundation 76
Najmiyeh Hospital 13, 50, 52, 54, 69-72, 75-76, 101
Naraghi, Ehsan 58
Nassiri, Nematollah (Gen.) 26, 45, 109-111
National Council of Security 15
National Iranian Airways 57
National Iranian Oil Company 103
National Tourist Organization 44, 65
navy 15, 82
New Zealand 54

O
oil products, increase in domestic price 103-106

P
Pahlavi Foundation 64
Pahlavi, Ashraf (Princess) 90, 92

Pahlavi, Farah (Queen) 41, 48, 87-89, 93-96, 98, 121, 126
Pahlavi, Mohammad-Reza Shah 15-16, 18-19, 24-25, 34-35, 39-42, 46-49, 53, 56, 62, 66-68, 78, 81-82, 84-85, 89-90, 92-93, 97, 100, 103, 105-107, 110-111, 114, 116-124, 126-128, 141
Pahlavi, Reza Shah 17-18, 50, 55-56, 64, 73
Pahlavi, Shahnaz 85
Pahlavi, Shams (Princess) 81, 87, 90
Pahlbod, Mehrdad 44, 68, 90
Pakistan 13-14, 19, 57, 68, 80, 93-95, 109, 114, 117
Pakravan, Emineh 53, 81, 84-85, 87, 91, 115
Pakravan, Fathollah.. 17, 55-57, 64
Pakravan, Saideh 88
Panama 48
Park Hotel 75-76
Pension Saint Honoré d'Eylau 50
Persian Gulf ports and harbors 27
Persian language 69
Philip (Prince) 89
Philippines... 109
Poitiers artillery school 18
Poles 50, 77
police 15, 45, 113
Poona, India 85
prison... 27, 38, 73, 128, 131-32
Prix Rivarol 53
propaganda 38, 43, 68, 96, 105, 112
Pryor, Geoffrey 28

Q
queen of England 89

R
radio 33, 46-47
Raji, Abdolhossein (Dr.) 54
Rampour, India 82
Razmara, Haj-Ali (Gen.) 80
RCD 21, 23
Red Lion & Sun Association of Iran................................ 58, 90

Rezai, Ghassem 65-66
Roghani, -- (Haj) 42-43
Rome 57, 66, 78
rumors 16, 86-87, 97-98, 111, 117-119
Russia 15, 50, 54-56, 60-61, 77, 109

S
Sabeti, Parviz 26, 115-117
Sadabad Palace 81
Saleh, Allahyar 27
San Antonio, Texas 48
SAVAK .... See State Intelligence and Security Organization
security 16, 19-20, 25-26, 104
Shah Abdolazim, shrine of 31
Shah Cheragh, shrine of 31
Shahvand palace 81
Shariatmadari, Mohammad-Kazem (Ayatollah Seyyed). 30, 40
Sheibani, Mehdi 65-66
Sicard, -- (Professor) 45
Sikhs 54
Society for the Protection of Animals 58
State Intelligence and Security Organization (SAVAK) 15, 20, 25, 26, 33, 35-36, 41, 45-47, 65, 87, 97, 103-104, 106-107, 110, 113, 114, 133
Stodach, -- (Gen.) 58, 113
students 61-62
Switzerland 19, 52, 92

T
technocrats 104-105
Tehrani, Jalal (Seyyed) 40
television 46
Tiflis, Georgia 50
torture 26
Tourist Organization 64-68, 91
tribal organizations 28
Twenty-eighth of Mordad 1332 16
Tudeh Party 15

Turkey 23-24, 41

U
United Nations 67
United Nations Conference on Tourism 66-67
University of Tehran 53, 58, 61

V
Vatican 55
veil 30, 50
violence 107-108
Vossough, Ali 80
Vossough, Hassan (Vossough al-Dowleh) 79
Vossoughi, Jahangir (Dr.) 72

W
World War II 51, 53, 55, 60

Y
Yazdanpanah, Morteza (Gen.) 83, 99-100

Z
Zahedi, Ardeshir 118
Zahedi, Fazlollah (Gen.) 81

۱۲۲	آخرین روزهای حکومت سلطنتی
۱۲۵	بازداشت امیر عباس هویدا
۱۳۰	بازداشت و اعدام سرلشکر پاکروان

پیوست‌ها

۱۳۵	۱: فهرست روایت کنندگان
۱۴۲	۲: اسامی همکاران طرح تاریخ شفاهی ایران
۱۴۳	۳: اسامی کتابخانه هایی که مجموعه تاریخ شفاهی ایران را در اختیار دارند
۱۴۵	فهرست راهنما

۵۰	جلسه دوم: ۷ مارس ۱۹۸۳ (۱۶ اسفند ۱۳۶۱)
۵۰	سوابق خانوادگی و تحصیلی فاطمه پاکروان
۵۲	خدمت در بیمارستان نجمیه
۵۵	فتح الله پاکروان، پدر سرلشکر پاکروان
۵۷	خدمت در شرکت هواپیمائی ایران
۵۸	خدمات اجتماعی
۶۳	سازمان جلب سیاحان ایران
۶۸	سفیر ایران در پاکستان (۴۷-۱۳۴۵)
۶۹	دوره دوم در بیمارستان نجمیه
۷۹	احمد قوام السلطنه
۸۰	سرلشکر حاجعلی رزم آرا
۸۱	ثریا، ملکه سابق
۸۶	محیط دربار شاهنشاهی
۸۷	شهبانو فرح، دوران اول
۹۰	شاهدخت اشرف پهلوی
۹۳	شهبانو فرح، دوران بعدی
۹۸	حسین علاء
۱۰۱	دکتر منوچهر اقبال
۱۰۳	اختلاف نظر در مورد افزایش قیمت بنزین
۱۰۴	روی کار آمدن تکنوکرات ها
۱۰۶	افزایش قیمت نفت و بنزین
۱۰۶	ترورهای دهه ۱۳۵۰
۱۱۰	ارتشبد نعمت الله نصیری
۱۱۲	برخورد مردم با همسر رئیس سازمان امنیت
۱۱۴	جریان قتل در کفاشی شارل ژوردن
۱۱۷	انتصاب سرلشکر پاکروان در وزارت دربار
۱۲۰	آخرین ملاقاتهای سرلشکر پاکروان با شاه

فهرست مطالب

۱	مقدمه
۳	شرح حال مختصر فاطمه پاکروان
۴	شرح حال سرلشکر حسن پاکروان
۵	معرفی خاطرات فاطمه پاکروان
۱۰	فضای گفت و گو
۱۱	طرح تاریخ شفاهی ایران
۱۲	املای اسامی اشخاص
۱۳	**خاطرات فاطمه پاکروان**
۱۳	جلسه اول: ۳ مارس ۱۹۸۳ (۱۲ اسفند ۱۳۶۱)
۱۷	تحصیلات مقدماتی سرلشکر پاکروان
۱۸	کودتای ۲۸ مرداد ۱۳۳۲
۱۹	تاسیس سازمان اطلاعات و امنیت کشور
۲۱	سپهبد تیمور بختیار
۲۳	انتصاب پاکروان به ریاست سازمان امنیت
۲۹	قیام ۱۵ خرداد ۱۳۴۲
۳۶	بازداشت آیت الله خمینی
۳۸	نجات آیت الله خمینی از مرگ
۴۴	قتل حسنعلی منصور، نخست وزیر
۴۵	انتصاب سرلشکر پاکروان به وزارت اطلاعات
۴۷	عکس العمل شاه نسبت به اعدام سرلشکر پاکروان

این کتاب توسط مرکز مطالعات خاورمیانه دانشگاه هاروارد منتشر و به وسیله کتابفروشی ایران

8014 Georgetown Road

Bethesda, MD 20814 USA

تلفن ۸۱۸۸-۷۱۸-۳۰۱   فاکس ۸۷۰۷-۹۰۷-۳۰۱

توزیع می شود.

مجموعه تاریخ شفاهی ایران
۶

خاطرات
فاطمه پاکروان

همسر سرلشکر حسن پاکروان: افسر ارتش،
رئیس سازمان اطلاعات و امنیت کشور،
وزیر اطلاعات و سفیر

ویراستار
حبیب لاجوردی

طرح تاریخ شفاهی ایران
مرکز مطالعات خاورمیانه
دانشگاه هاروارد
۱۹۹۸

خاطرات فاطمه پاکروان

www.ingramcontent.com/pod-product-compliance
Lightning Source LLC
Chambersburg PA
CBHW021832300426
44114CB00009BA/406